MAGNIFYING GOD'S WORD

SERMONS BY GEORGE L. GLASS SR.

MAGNIFYING

GOD'S WORD

COMPILED BY MYRTISE F. GLASS

Magnifying God's Word

Sermons by George L. Glass, Sr.
Compiled by Myrtise F. Glass

©1992 Word Aflame Press
  Hazelwood, MO 63042-2299

Cover Design by Tim Agnew

Printed in United States of America.

Printed by

Library of Congress Cataloging-in-Publication Data

Glass, George L., 1909-1990.
    Magifying God's word / sermons by George Glass; compiled by Myrtise F. Glass.
          p.   cm.
      ISBN 0-932581-49-8
      1. United Pentecostal Church International—Sermons.
    2. Pentecostal churches—Sermons. 3. Sermons—Outlines, syllabi, etc. 4. Sermons, American. I. Glass, Myrtise F., 1914-
    II. Title.
    BX8780.Z6G42   1992
    252'.0994—dc20   92-11978
                                                              CIP

To the membership of the United Pentecostal Church International, to the memory of those who have served in God's work and passed on, and to those who are yet to come in His service. May the pages and voice of one gone to his reward bring inspiration to you. May we always respond in obedient faith to God's goodness, grace, and abundant love toward us.

CONTENTS

Foreword 9

Preface 11

Biography of George Glass, Sr. 15

1. Figures and Facts 19

2. The Far-Reaching Effects of
Saul's Incomplete Obedience 41

3. Back to Bethel 51

4. Satan Among the Saints................... 77

5. Thou Hast Magnified Thy Word above Thy Name 97

6. The Accuracy of God's Word............... 121

7. Defeating the Enemy with His Own Weapon ..143

8. Equal Chance 177

Foreword

He was an epic in his time. Like Goliath's sword, there has never been another like him. He was my pastor, my mentor, my friend—George Glass, Sr.—prince of preachers.

What a privilege it is for me to speak of this giant of the faith. Many of you who will give perusal to this book knew him as a conference and camp meeting preacher. I knew him intimately as a friend. I was asked once what, to me, was the most outstanding factor in the life of George Glass, Sr. I immediately replied, "Above all else, he was a Christian." It was my privilege to walk with him through the highest mountains of his successful pastoral and organizational work. It was also my loving duty to walk with him during the darkest valleys of his life. And believe me, he had some dark valleys.

Whenever you hear sermons of George Glass or read them in this book, you are drinking from a well of experience. This man walked what he preached. He would often say, "You cannot talk that talk if you don't walk that walk." Many of the sermons herein I personally heard him preach. Print could never reproduce the verbal anointing.

No, there will never be another like him. Maybe I am prejudiced, but, to me, he was the greatest! I commend to you the works of George Glass, Sr.—Christian par excellence. I still miss him.

T. F. Tenney
District Superintendent, Louisiana

Preface

For years I tried to get Brother Glass to put some sermons in a book. He was too modest, sincerely and honestly modest, to consider this. After many others spoke to him about a book, he finally said to me, "When I am gone, do what you wish to with my sermon outlines, tapes, and notes." This is the result. The dedication explains why I wished to print a book.

This book does not contain many of Brother Glass's better-known exhortations. If you have derived any good from my portrayal of these messages, I would like to hear from you, thus letting me know whether I should attempt another.

I wish to express thanks to the following people for transcribing tapes for me:

Lucille Barnhill
Mary Cheatham
Terry Cheever
Kristi Craft
Linda Crain
Karla Christian
Ersula Flaherty
Darla Solinsky
Ilena Storozyszyn

I am deeply in debt to Terry Cheever for allowing me to use her as a "listening post" and hearing me out when I just had to ask someone, "How does this wording sound? Is it clear?"

Many evangelists, when preaching for different churches that Brother Glass pastored, would stay up at night to duplicate his notebook. He never withheld anything from anyone who wanted what he had. He always said, "God can dry up the source," if he were to develop a selfish attitude. God had given freely to him, so he felt he should be free with what he had.

Someone said, "The average preacher will cross the world to preach a sermon but will not cross the street to hear one." Nevertheless, Brother Glass became known as "the preacher's preacher."

When called to minister to the general board and various departments of our organization, he felt inadequate and unqualified. He was driven to his knees to intercede for the "right word, the right message for my ministering brethren."

After hearing one of our renowned ministers preach he said to me, "I feel like Ned in the third reader. Just think, we ministered in his pastorate to his people!"

When he was approached about teaching the graduating ministerial students in one of our Bible colleges, we had difficulty in convincing him that he was qualified. Once he was into the preparation of lessons to teach to them, however, he realized the potential before him. He ended up with many notes. We outlined and typed them for him, and they ended up being the length of a book.

Somehow a teacher in another of our colleges came into possession of the written lessons or part of them. We received a call from him wanting to use the chapter on weddings. Of course it was okay. In the background I reminded Brother Glass to tell the teacher we were going to use the material for a book. His answer: "Oh, well, if it is good for one, it will be good in another." Very meekly I prepared and mailed the lesson to our caller and very dear friend.

Brother Glass allowed no man to be his enemy. "If they make me their enemy that is between them and God. I have no enemies."

He turned down no opening Jesus offered to him. He tried everything in various places of service to his God. In one year of 365 days, he preached 465 times. From those sermons 729 received the Holy Ghost.

He was truly a man "in whom there is no guile." He was also a man of prayer.

My desire is in some way to catch and portray the heart of this man, so that others will be moved to set their course for Jesus.

Myrtise F. Glass
(Mrs. George L. Glass, Sr.)

Biography of George Glass, Sr.

In January 1933, at the age of twenty-three years, George L. Glass, Sr. began a ministry that grew and enlarged until the demands of that ministry enabled him to become acquainted with and drawn into every facet of the United Pentecostal Church International work and outreach.

Brother Glass's first pastorate was at Bethel Grove, near DeRidder, Louisiana, in 1933. From that time he was actively engaged in full-time ministry. In 1934, he accepted the pastorate of First Pentecostal Church in Many, Louisiana, and in 1936, he accepted the pastorate of Faith Tabernacle, Port Arthur, Texas.

During his pastoral years, Brother Glass also served in several organizational positions. He was elected secretary-treasurer of the South Central Association of the Pentecostal Churches, Inc. for 1936-38. In 1938 he was elected superintendent while continuing to pastor the Port Arthur congregation. The late A. T. Morgan was a member of the district board.

Brother Glass resigned the superintendency of the South Central Association of the Pentecostal Churches, Inc. in 1940 but was elected to serve the organization as secretary-treasurer, while also continuing pastoral duties. After the merger that formed the United Pentecostal Church, Brother Glass served as the secretary-treasurer of the Louisiana District for twenty-two years. He was one of the leaders who labored many hours to help formulate the constitution of the United Pentecostal Church International.

Brother Glass was called to pastor his home church in DeRidder, Louisiana, in 1945. While there, church growth demanded building a new church. After its completion he was led of the Spirit to pray, "Lord, let the world feel the effect of this little church." The record proves that the world has felt the effect of this church. Under Brother Glass's influence the church grew in numbers. It also increased in monetary giving, much of which was directed to foreign missions. Many ministers came up under him to become pastors, evangelists, board members, and one of our foreign missions directors.

Also during the year of 1945, Brother Glass was appointed to serve as associate foreign missions director for the United Pentecostal Church, serving along with the director, Wynn Stairs. He held this position for eleven years.

A radio station began broadcasting in DeRidder, Louisiana, in 1950. The DeRidder First Pentecostal Church had the first broadcast aired on this station and still maintains that spot with the station. During all his pastorates Brother Glass carried on an active radio ministry.

In 1953, Brother Glass accepted the pastorate of the First Pentecostal Church of Baton Rouge, Louisiana, and in 1956, he was elected to serve as home missions director in the United States and Canada.

During 1950 Tupelo Children's Mansion was founded. Brother Glass was active in this endeavor and served on the board of directors.

Brother Glass resigned as home missions director in 1958 and accepted the pastorate of First Pentecostal Church, formerly known as Bible Hour Tabernacle, in Jonesboro, Arkansas. In 1962, he went to pastor Bemis

Pentecostal Church in Jackson, Tennessee. Because of his love for and interest in foreign missions work, he visited Jamaica to strengthen the churches there. In March 1968 he resigned the Bemis church and became a full-time evangelist.

July 1970 found Brother Glass back at his home church in DeRidder and involved in an extensive building program.

In February 1972 the Foreign Missions Division sent the Glasses to minister in Tokyo, the Philippine Islands, and Hawaii. In Manila, Brother Glass was speaker for the first Southwestern Pacific and Asian regional missionary conference of the United Pentecostal Church. Brother Glass began attending the School of Missions of the Foreign Missions Division in 1972 as devotional speaker. He continued as devotional speaker until his death.

After resigning the pastorate of the DeRidder church, the Glasses continued to teach the adult Bible class when at home. During this time they also drove to Houston, Texas, on Mondays and taught four classes on Tuesday and Thursday at Texas Bible College.

During his lifetime Brother Glass served in the following positions: evangelist, pastor, district superintendent, district secretary-treasurer, associate foreign missions director, Tupelo Children's Mansion board member, general home missions director, camp meeting speaker (having preached in seventy-five to one hundred camp meetings), radio speaker, devotional speaker at the School of Missions, teacher at Texas Bible College, speaker abroad for the Foreign Missions Division, and interim pastor to several churches after his resignation from active pastorate. He attended all but two general conferences of the

United Pentecostal Church International.

Brother Glass departed from this life on Saturday evening, March 17, 1990. He was truly a "giant among men."

1

FIGURES AND FACTS
Matthew 21:23-27

Outline

Introduction: Man figures. He always has. But God is a God of facts.

   I. Adam and Eve (Genesis 3:6-13)
      A. Sewed fig leaves for aprons
      B. Hid themselves
      C. God brought them face to face with facts

   II. Achan (Joshua 7:1)
      A. He figured—hid his spoil in his tent
      B. The consequences

   III. David (II Samuel 11:1)
      A. He was smooth at figuring
      B. God brought him face to face with facts he created

   IV. Birth of Jesus
      A. Herod figured how to get rid of Him
      B. Men figured how to get rid of Jesus during His ministry
      C. Nicodemus figured
      D. Jesus' resurrection
      E. Day of Pentecost—men figured the disciples were drunk
      F. Ananias and Sapphira figured
      G. The barn builder figured

V. People Are Still Figuring Today

Conclusion: People are able to figure their way through this life. Many times they ease their conscience by figuring their way around, or through, things. But God will eventually bring them face to face with facts.

FIGURES AND FACTS

And when he was come into the temple, the chief priests and the elders of the people came unto him as he was teaching, and said, By what authority doest thou these things? and who gave thee this authority? And Jesus answered and said unto them, I will also ask you one thing, which if ye tell me, I in like wise will tell by what authority I do these things. The baptism of John, whence was it? from heaven, or of men? And they reasoned with themselves, saying, If we say, From heaven, he will say unto us, Why did ye not then believe him? But if we say, Of men, we fear the people; for all hold John as a prophet. And they answered Jesus, and said, We cannot tell. And he said unto them, Neither tell I you by what authority I do these things (Matthew 21:23-27).

These verses introduce the thought that we want to discuss: figures and facts. There is a difference between "figures and facts" and "facts and figures." We can try to figure around facts, but God will always bring us back to facts! Always!

The foregoing passage of Scripture beautifully portrays this truth. Some people came to Jesus as He was ministering in the Temple. They asked Him, "By what authority do you do these things?"

Jesus answered, "I'm going to ask you a question." Let us notice the wisdom Jesus used. Many times He answered questions by another question that rendered the first question ineffectual. Speaking of John the Baptist, Jesus asked His critics, "What about the baptism of John, was it of God, or was it of men?"

Instantly they started trying to figure around the facts! They were smooth and keen. In fact, we could say they were astute of mind, shrewd, and sharp in their figuring. They said among themselves, "If we say the baptism of John was of God, He will say, 'Well, why didn't you follow Him?' If we say the baptism of John was not of God, but was of men, then we will be in trouble with the people, for they consider John a prophet." They figured well and concluded by answering, "We can't tell you." Did they mean "We can't tell" or "We won't tell"? They tried to figure around the facts but could not change the facts!

Jesus said, "Neither will I tell you by what authority I do these things." He really was saying, "If you won't answer me, I won't answer you." In essence, He let them know that He understood the nature and substance of their reasoning. They figured well, but they did not change the facts.

We live in a world of knowledgeable people who are astute at figuring out things, even to the extent of conquering space. Many people have laid aside the Bible and ignore God, but God is going to bring us face to face with facts. Figures will be laid aside! Let us look at examples of this truth from God's Word.

We will start in Genesis 3 with the record of the first people who sinned. In the beautiful Garden of Eden, paradise on earth, Adam and Eve transgressed the law of God. After their disobedience, the former innocents found themselves naked in their sight, and more importantly, unclothed in God's sight. The blight of sin caused them to feel corrupt, depraved, tainted, and infected with error. They immediately began figuring what to do.

Humanity has been figuring around facts ever since, but figuring has never changed facts with God.

Adam and Eve figured and concluded, "Here's a beautiful fig tree. We will take some of these big, green, thick leaves and pin them together to make us clothes." After doing that they still did not feel comfortable with their fig-leaf garments. They figured further and decided, "We will hide from God."

We can never hide from God. No one has ever hidden himself from God. It can't be done! Adam and Eve thought they were hidden until the Lord came along and called out, "Adam, where are you?" Adam and Eve had to come out of hiding to stand in the presence of God, dressed in their fig leaves. They had to confess what they had done. They were not sufficiently clothed until an animal was slain and God clothed them in His own God-given garments!

Adam's figuring did not change one thing with God. He had to face facts! "Unto Adam also and to his wife did the LORD God make coats of skin, and clothed them" (Genesis 3:21). Before the skins could be obtained an animal had to be slain. "Without shedding of blood is no remission" (Hebrews 9:22). The coats of skin were divinely provided garments that the first sinners might be made fit for God's presence, and as such they are a type of Christ, "who of God is made unto us . . . righteousness" (I Corinthians 1:30).

A few books further in the Bible, we find a God-given law. It was not given by Joshua. It was not given by Moses. God decided to give the Israelites the city of Jericho. The Israelites were in no position to charge through the wall. All they had to do was march around

25

the city as God instructed. The Lord would cause the walls to fall flat before them so that they could take it. But there were some restrictions!

Why there were restrictions is not our subject now. There was a restriction to Adam and Eve in the garden: "Let that tree alone. Don't eat of its fruit." Likewise, in Jericho the Israelites had restrictions to obey. "The city shall be accursed, even it, and all that are therein" (Joshua 6:17). God's law further stated that upon taking Jericho the Israelites were to put all the silver, gold, brass, and iron into the treasury of the Lord (Joshua 6:19).

Upon the conquest of Jericho, one man in the army, Achan, allowed his eyes to feast upon the gold, silver, and Babylonian clothes. Achan immediately started figuring. I want—I want that garment! I want that wedge of gold! What can I do? What do I want with it? What can I do with it? Well, I don't know. I guess maybe it could be just because God said, "Leave it alone."

We should not be surprised at how our Adamic nature moves us to want to do something that God tells us not to do. A father of five children related that he tried to keep from telling his children not to do something. He had observed the children's reaction to his words. "Don't do that" caused them to want to try it. He tried to train them, set an example, and teach them to do right without telling them not to do something.

Have you ever observed people reading a sign that says, "Don't touch! Wet paint." The normal reaction of most people is to touch and see. Can't they believe the sign means what it says? The reason we want to do things contrary to the teaching of the law of God is that the old Adamic nature, if permitted, will motivate us to do what we really do not want to do.

Perhaps Achan did not see anything wrong with the Babylonian garment. We do not know exactly what kind of garment it was, whether it was long or short, full or tight, heavy or light, thick or thin, or even its color. What made it sin? God said, "Leave it alone." That made it sin!

Let us digress long enough to say this: Pentecostal ministers are sometimes accused of being clothesline preachers. We can cite passages of Scripture that give ministers the authority to teach on clothes, but that is not our present subject. One minister said he had no idea as to what the forbidden fruit was that made Adam and Eve realize they were unclothed, but if he did know, after observing people in public in various stages of undress, he would certainly buy and pass around baskets of the fruit to wake some people up!

Achan figured out what he was going to do: I've got a tent. I'll take the garment, gold, and silver, and bury them in my tent! But all that he touched was controlled and governed by God's law. Because of Achan's covetousness he became inordinately desirous of the forbidden. He lusted after the money and garment. "Then when lust hath conceived, it bringeth forth sin: and sin, when it is finished, bringeth forth death" (James 1:15). Achan's confession was, "I coveted" (Joshua 7:21). He had ignored the commandment "Thou shalt not covet" (Exodus 20:17) as well as the instruction on this occasion to let the accursed thing alone.

Somehow Achan figured out a way to conceal the garment, gold, and silver in order to get them to his tent. Achan dug a hole in the earth, the floor of his tent, and placed the gold, silver, and garment within. After smoothing the dirt evenly, he probably spread skin rugs or Oriental carpet over the place. He felt the contraband was successfully and neatly hidden away with no one in all the world knowing anything about it. It was all stashed away for a rainy day or a special occasion.

That was shrewd thinking to Achan. But what good did it do him? If he spent the money people would question where he got so much. What good did the garment do him? He never got to wear it! To make a long story short, God, in His unquestionable wisdom uncovered it. Achan, like Adam and Eve, had to confess his sin. He not only lost his life, but his family also paid the consequences. (See Joshua 7:24-25.)

God's Word reveals to us the folly of giving up God for earthly desires. What good did Judas Iscariot's thirty pieces of silver do for him? Remorse ate away at his conscience until he hanged himself, and was buried in a potter's field bought with the thirty pieces of silver (Matthew 27:3-8).

In II Samuel 11-12 we read of some of the smoothest figuring a man ever did. Nowhere in God's Word do we read of any one more cunning, more skillful and crafty and better at figuring around the facts than King David. But this man too, though a king, had to face facts!

It seems as though David should have been on the battlefield with his men at war, but he was not. Had he been where he ought to have been, he would not have been tempted. He was out of place! That is where most temptations come: when we are out of place. We may not be doing anything wrong yet, but we just do not feel right. When we are where we ought to be, we have a sweet consolation and can ask God to shield us. In our walk with

God, He teaches us to pray, "Lord, lead me not into temptation."

And it came to pass, after the year was expired, at the time when kings go forth to battle, that David sent Joab, and his servants with him, and all Israel. . . . But David tarried still at Jerusalem (II Samuel 11:1).

One evening David arose from his bed, walked upon the cool roof of the palace, and saw a woman bathing herself. The woman was very beautiful. David asked a servant to find out who she was. He was told she was Bathsheba, the wife of Uriah, who was away on the battlefront.

Bathsheba belonged to one of David's soldiers. That fact should have deterred his thoughts toward her. He knew the commandment "Thou shalt not commit adultery" (Exodus 20:14). In our day, people no longer respect this and many other commandments of God. Still, God's Word stands regarding this, and sooner or later, they will have to face facts!

David sent for Bathsheba and took her for himself. Soon after she returned home, he received word from her: "I am with child." What was he going to do now? No doubt he reflected back over his life to this point, remembering how God had blessed him down through the years at so many places and points in his life, until now he was not only king over Judah but king over all Israel. Perhaps he was very remorseful. But it was too late now. He had to face facts!

David tried to do some figuring. He planned very smoothly. He sent a message to Joab saying, "Send me

Uriah." He was king; he had the authority to do this. When Uriah came, David inquired of him, "How is Joab? How are the soldiers doing? Is the war going in our favor?" These were questions that any king would ask regarding his men, not questions that would betray his motives. Anyone would be interested in the things he asked about. After receiving the report, David told Uriah to take a few days of furlough, to go home and visit his wife. He even sent a gift of meat.

But Uriah slept at the door of the king's house with all the servants of his lord, and went not down to his house. And when they had told David, saying, Uriah went not down unto his house, David said unto Uriah, Camest thou not from thy journey? Why then didst thou not go down unto thine house? And Uriah said unto David, The ark, and Israel, and Judah, abide in tents; and my lord Joab, and the servants of my lord, are encamped in the open fields; shall I then go into mine house, to eat and to drink, and to lie with my wife? as thou liveth, and as thy soul liveth, I will not do this thing (II Samuel 11:9-11).

What a surprise! David had not reckoned on such loyalty as this. Many times we wonder how saints can forget about revival and stay home when their church is waging spiritual warfare against the enemy for the souls of their loved ones, friends, and acquaintances. They should consider the loyalty of Uriah to his fellow soldiers. God's Word exhorts us: "Not forsaking the assembling of ourselves together, as the manner of some is; but exhorting one another: and so much the more, as ye see the day approaching" (Hebrews 10:25).

David's figuring did not work out as he thought it would. He figured out a further plan: He decided to honor Uriah with the privilege of drinking with the king. Any soldier in any army would feel honored if he could sit and drink with the king.

And when David had called him, he did eat and drink before him; and he made him drunk: and at even he went out to lie on his bed with the servants of his lord, but went not to his house (II Samuel 11:13).

David could not make Uriah forget loyalty and patriotism even though he was drunken. What now, David? So David figured out the ultimate tragedy in the life of a good soldier. David wrote a letter to Joab. The king had authority on his side. He could order anything he wanted and it would be done.

And it came to pass in the morning that David wrote a letter to Joab, and sent it by the hand of Uriah. He wrote in the letter, saying, Set ye Uriah in the forefront of the hottest battle, and retire ye from him, that he may be smitten, and die (II Samuel 11:14-15).

What a tragic, pitiful picture! Can we see the innocent, loyal, faithful, patriotic Uriah carrying his own death warrant in his hand? Uriah was an honest man. He never once thought of opening it. He could not, for it carried the king's seal. He had no reason to suspect, or expect, other than good from his king. He carried the letter safely and placed it in his captain's hand. Joab followed the king's orders and sent David word of what happened.

31

Like Uriah, you carry your fate in your own hands!
You have the destiny of your soul in your own hands! It
is not in mine. It is not in your mother's. It is not in your
father's. Your destiny is in your own hands. You may
weep at the picture of Uriah carrying his letter of destiny,
but that is where you are—walking along the road of
life . . . searching . . . looking . . . expecting. . . . If you
are picking up a trivial dish of pottage, partaking of it,
selling your birthright, and sacrificing your soul, as Esau,
then you are more pathetic and pitiful than Uriah. You
will lose not only your life but also your soul.

*And when the wife of Uriah heard that Uriah her hus-
band was dead, she mourned for her husband. And when
the mourning was past, David sent and fetched her to his
house, and she became his wife, and bare him a son* (II Samuel 11:26-27).

David figured it all out. Now it was all over. Nobody
would ever know. But wait, David. You have momentarily
forgotten. God knows all! He alone knows all the figuring that has gone on in the mind and hearts of people,
and it will not stand up any more than David's did!

Time marched on. All was past and seemingly forgotten. Amid peace and quiet, David sat upon his throne,
reigning and ruling as king. Everything, he thought, was
taken care of, until God sent Nathan, His prophet, to
David.

Nathan said, "David, there is a rich man in your
kingdom who has many flocks and herds. Also in the
kingdom is a poor man who had one little lamb, only one.
The rich man had a guest come to see him. Instead of kill-

ing one of his own sheep, he took the poor man's one little ewe lamb, killed it, prepared it, and served it to his guest. What about this, David?"

David felt very secure. He did not realize that he would judge himself. Jesus said, "Judge not, that ye be not judged. For with what judgment ye judge, ye shall be judged: and with what measure ye mete, it shall be measured to you again" (Matthew 7:1-2). That law will never change.

David's anger was greatly kindled against the man; and he said to Nathan, As the LORD liveth, the man that has done this thing shall surely die: and he shall restore the lamb fourfold, because he did this thing, and because he had no pity. And Nathan said to David, Thou art the man! . . . Wherefore hast thou despised the commandment of the LORD, to do evil in his sight? thou hast killed Uriah . . . and taken his wife. . . . Now therefore the sword shall never depart from thine house. . . . And David said unto Nathan, I have sinned against the LORD. . . . And Nathan said unto David, . . . The child also that is born unto thee shall surely die (II Samuel 12:5-7, 9-10, 13-14).

David spent the rest of his life in remorse and repentance. He had to learn to live with his guilt. The extent of his suffering is revealed in Psalm 51, the prayer of a murderer. He could not figure around his sin.

God always brings the sinner face to face with facts! This is always the result. It always will be. All the way through God's Word people have continued to figure, but not around facts. They eventually have to face the judgment of God.

In Matthew 2 we read that King Herod ruled in Jerusalem at the time of Jesus' birth. Three wise men from the East came asking, "Where is he that is born King of the Jews? for we have seen his star in the east, and are come to worship him" (Matthew 2:2).

When King Herod heard this he was troubled. What does this mean? he wondered. I'm king of the Jews! When he had gathered all of the chief priests and scribes together, he demanded of them where Christ should be born. They told him what the prophets had written: in Bethlehem of Judea would come a governor to rule Israel.

Herod was now troubled even more. The wise men's story had the ring of truth. The prophets had written about this. Herod had the facts before him. He decided to do some figuring.

But Herod could not outfigure God. All his counselors, his ability, and all the strategy he had ever used in war, law, or order would not work. Nevertheless he figured: I'll tell them that when they find the baby born king of the Jews to come back and let me know. I want to go worship him! God knew his secret figuring, and God was always a step ahead, never behind or too late.

God spoke to the wise men to go back another way. Herod waited, but they did not return. When Herod realized he was mocked by the wise men, he was exceedingly angry. He began to figure how long had it been since they had been there. He found that several months had gone by, and he began to wonder how long the baby had been born before they came. He figured it out: To be safe I'll have every male child under the age of two put to death. That will get him! But no, Herod, that was just your figuring.

34

God spoke to Joseph: "Take Mary and the baby down into Egypt, and stay there until I tell you to return, for Herod will seek the young child to destroy him." Herod killed all those babies, but failed in his figuring. The fact is, God is always ahead of the enemy.

This is an evil day. People say hard things about God, the church, and His people, never realizing they are fulfilling Scripture. Let us remember: God reigns! He is in control. One day soon He will say it is enough! Then the facts will stand!

Are you one who is afraid of facts? A certain man was on trial for stealing, and he was very nervous. Someone told him not to be so jittery: "Don't you know the judge will give you justice?" The man replied, "That's what I'm afraid of."

In the stillness of a dark night, a good man by the name of Nicodemus went to Jesus and said, "Rabbi, we know that thou art a teacher come from God: for no man can do these miracles that thou doest, except God be with him" (John 3:2).

Jesus answered him, "You must be born again." Now let us watch that man start figuring. "How can a man be born when he is old?" Jesus said, "Do not marvel, Nicodemus. You understand the fleshly birth, but I want you to understand the spiritual birth. You must be born again. You are a teacher in Israel and don't know these facts?" Nicodemus's figuring still has not changed the facts. That message is just as real as it ever was. "Ye must be born again" (John 3:7).

After Jesus was crucified and laid in the tomb, the chief priests and Pharisees had an uneasy feeling. They figured they had better do something. Their figuring moved them to action!

35

Now the next day, that followed the day of the prepara-tion, the chief priests and Pharisees came together unto Pilate, Saying, Sir, we remember that that deceiver said, while he was yet alive, After three days I will rise again. Command therefore that the sepulchre be made sure until the third day, lest his disciples come by night, and steal him away, and say unto the people, He is risen from the dead: so the last error shall be worse than the first. Pilate said unto them, Ye have a watch: go your way, make it as sure as ye can. So they went, and made the sepulchre sure, sealing the stone, and setting a watch (Matthew 27:62-66).

They placed a guard to do what? To prevent the seal from being tampered with, the stone from being removed, or the dead man's body from being stolen away?

There is no louder proclamation to the truth of Christ's death and resurrection than the guard at the empty tomb. The figuring of the Jewish religious leaders was for evil purposes. They did not see the hand of God moving to solidify the truth for time and eternity. No, they did not figure well, for their efforts only served as confirmation to divine facts!

The enemy hates to give up. When the guards real-ized what had taken place, they ran to tell the chief priests and Pharisees. When these men consulted with the elders they again figured what to do: If the news that He is risen gets out over the country, what is that going to do to us? The guards are the only witnesses, so we can bribe them. They gave large sums of money to the guards to tell that His disciples came by night and stole his body away. Again, they did not figure well at all. They just enlarged the guard's pay and figured themselves out of much money. They figured and paid but did not move facts! He lives!

Before ascending on high Jesus told the disciples to tarry in Jerusalem until they were endued with power from on high (Luke 24:49). The Day of Pentecost found the disciples tarrying, worshiping, and praising God.

And when the day of Pentecost was fully come, they were all with one accord in one place. And suddenly there came a sound from heaven as of a rushing mighty wind, and it filled all the house where they were sitting. And there appeared unto them cloven tongues like as of fire, and it sat upon each of them. And they were all filled with the Holy Ghost, and began to speak with other tongues as the Spirit gave them utterance (Acts 2:1-4).

The news of this event spread all over the city. A multitude came together asking, "What does this mean?" They started trying to figure it out. Some mockers said, "These men are full of new wine. They are drunk!"

Peter explained, "This is what was spoken by the prophet Joel." He referred to facts. Figuring cannot explain away the facts of God.

Another example of a man's figuring is the story of the barn builder in the parable of the rich fool in Luke 12:16-21.

And he [Jesus] spake a parable unto them, saying, The ground of a certain rich man brought forth plentifully: and he thought within himself, saying, What shall I do, because I have no room where to bestow my fruits? And he said, This will I do: I will pull down my barns, and build greater: and there will I bestow all my fruits and goods. And I will say to my soul, Soul, thou hast much goods laid up for many years; take thine ease, eat, drink, and be merry. But God said unto him, Thou fool, this night thy soul shall be required of thee: then whose shall those things be, which thou hast provided? So is he that layeth up treasure for himself, and is not rich toward God.

We cannot say anything against this man's business ability. He figured well in his business and was very successful. We cannot say anything against his morals. The Scripture does not tell us. We do find that his farm brought forth plentifully. His storage was overflowing. He had to build larger barns to take care of his goods. We do not know how many nights he stayed up figuring, or how much sleep he lost to arrive at his success.

What is wrong with this picture? In all his planning and figuring for success, he left God completely out of his life, a very foolish thing for a good businessman to do. He reveled in his success, thinking, I've got much goods laid up, enough for many years. This is what I've striven and fought for. Soul, take your ease, eat, drink, be merry, enjoy your success. You have earned it. But God called him a fool. The man had to face facts. Likewise, we will not figure a way around facing God to give account for our soul.

For our last example of "figures and facts," we go to Acts 4:32-5:11:

And the multitude of them that believed were of one heart and of one soul: neither said any of them that ought of the things which he possessed was his own; but they had all things common. And with great power gave the apostles witness of the resurrection of the Lord Jesus: and great grace was upon them all. Neither was there any among them that lacked: for as many as were possessors of lands or houses sold them, and brought the prices of the things that were sold, and laid them down at the apostles' feet: and distribution was made unto every man according as he had need. And Joses, who by the apostles was surnamed Barnabas, (which is, being interpreted, The son of consolation,) a Levite, and of the country of Cyprus, having land, sold it, and brought the money, and laid it at the apostles' feet.

But a certain man named Ananias, with Sapphira his wife, sold a possession. And kept back part of the price, his wife also being privy to it, and brought a certain part and laid it at the apostles' feet. But Peter said, Ananias, why hath Satan filled thine heart to lie to the Holy Ghost, and to keep back part of the price of the land? Whiles it remained, was it not thine own? and after it was sold, was it not in thine own power? why hast thou conceived this thing in thine heart? thou hast not lied unto men, but unto God. And Ananias hearing these words fell down, and gave up the ghost: and great fear came on all them that heard these things. And the young men arose, wound him up, and carried him out, and buried him. And it was about the space of three hours after, when his wife, not knowing what was done, came in. And Peter answered unto her, Tell me whether ye sold the land for so much? And she said, Yea, for so much. Then Peter said unto her, How is it that ye have agreed together to tempt the Spirit of the Lord? behold, the feet of them which have buried thy husband are at the door, and shall carry thee out. Then fell she down straightway at his feet, and yielded up the ghost: and the young men came in, and found her dead, and, carrying her forth, buried her by her husband. And great fear came upon all the church, and upon as many as heard these things.

Ananias and Sapphira wanted to appear to be as fully involved in the church as their brothers and sisters, yet hold onto part of their money while pretending to give all. They could have gotten by with this scheme had it not been for God's man.

Ananias and Sapphira agreed together in the privacy of their home to hold back part of the sale for their land and to say they were giving the total price of it. It was foolish figuring. They could pretend before people, but not with God.

Their hypocrisy resulted in their death. They did not go to hell from a bar or for neglecting church. They left from a church after figuring and sealing their doom. God called them to face facts.

We started in Genesis, went through the Law and the Prophets, through the Gospels, and into the Acts of the Apostles. We have shown how people down through time have tried to outfigure God. Nowhere has anyone ever figured and changed facts with God.

2

THE FAR-REACHING EFFECTS OF SAUL'S INCOMPLETE OBEDIENCE
I Samuel 15:13-16

Outline

Introduction: There is a difference between disobedience and incomplete obedience, but neither is acceptable to God. Few people realize the far-reaching effects of incomplete obedience.

  I. Incomplete Obedience Makes a Person Feel Good, But It Is Not Sufficient
   A. The example of Saul
   B. Saul destroyed Amalekites from Havilah to Shur
   C. He spared Agag and saved spoil for sacrifice
   D. His action was no substitute for obedience

 II. Saul's Incomplete Obedience Cost His Soul and More
   A. The blessing of God was taken from his household
   B. His sons could have been king after him
   C. The throne of Israel was given to another (I Samuel 15:28)
   D. The Amalekites were later destroyed by another (I Samuel 30:1-17)
   E. Saul died the death of a suicide (I Samuel 31:1-6)

III. Saul's Incomplete Obedience Affected God's Eternal Program
   A. God had promised Moses that He would put out the remembrance of Amalek and his people (Exodus 17:14)

B. Four hundred years later Saul was chosen to carry out God's promise
C. Saul's incomplete disobedience affected this promise
D. We are involved in the promise of God
E. The Old Testament saints "obtained a good report through faith, [but] received not the promise: God having provided some better thing for us, that they without us should not be made perfect" (Hebrews 11:39-40)

IV. God's Eternal Program Moves toward an Endless Eternity

THE FAR-REACHING EFFECTS OF SAUL'S INCOMPLETE OBEDIENCE

And Samuel came to Saul: and Saul said unto him, Blessed be thou of the LORD: I have performed the commandment of the LORD. And Samuel said, What meaneth then this bleating of the sheep in mine ears, and the lowing of the oxen which I hear? And Saul said, They have brought them from the Amalekites: for the people spared the best of the sheep and of the oxen, to sacrifice unto the LORD thy God; and the rest we have utterly destroyed. Then Samuel said unto Saul, Stay, and I will tell thee what the LORD hath said to me this night. And he said unto him, Say on (I Samuel 15:13-16).

There is a difference in disobedience and incomplete obedience, but neither is acceptable to God. Incomplete obedience has far-reaching effects!

We are not talking about the far-reaching effects of Saul's *dis*obedience. The subject is "the far-reaching effects of Saul's *incomplete* obedience." Incomplete obedience makes a person feel good in that he has at least partially obeyed, as was the case with Saul, but his incomplete obedience involved and affected a promise God made to Moses.

Four hundred years prior to Saul's action recorded in the foregoing passage of Scripture, Moses and the Israelites battled against the Amalekites (Exodus 17:8-14). On that occasion Moses told Joshua to take his army and meet the enemy in the valley. Moses stood at the top of the hill with the rod of God in his hand. Joshua was in the valley warring against the enemy. When Moses lifted up his hands, Joshua drove the enemy back. Then Moses' hands with the rod became heavy. When he let down his hands, the Amalekites prevailed. Moses lifted up his hands again, and Israel began to push the Amalekites back.

It was soon observed that when Moses' hands were up the Israelite were receiving victory, but when they were down Israel was being defeated. Aaron and Hur were convinced that the course of the battle depended upon whether Moses' hands were up or down. They went to the hilltop, took a stone, seated Moses on it, and stood on either side, steadying Moses' hands until the battle was won. How would the battle have gone had Aaron and Hur not seen the need and gone to lift up Moses' hands? Where there is a progressive church, the saints are holding up the pastor's hands and fully supporting the church.

The Lord told Moses, "Write this for a memorial in a book . . . I will utterly put out the remembrance of Amalek from under the heaven." God decreed that they no longer be a people, because the Amalekites, descendants of Esau, retarded the progress of Israel on their journey to the promised land.

In Saul's day God was now ready, even though four hundred years had passed, to keep His promise. "The Lord is not slack concerning his promise, as some men count slackness" (II Peter 3:9). He keeps His promises, and He uses others to keep the promises He has made.

Through Samuel God spoke to Saul, "Now go and smite Amalek, and utterly destroy all that they have, and spare not; but slay both man and woman; infant and suckling, ox and sheep, camel and ass" (I Samuel 15:3). Saul gathered his army and waited in the valley. He took time to tell the Kenites, "Go, depart, get you down from among the Amalekites, lest I destroy you with them: for ye shewed kindness to all the children of Israel, when they came up out of Egypt. So the Kenites departed from among the Amalekites" (I Samuel 15:6). There is a reason we teach separation from the world: the world is sure to be destroyed.

And Saul smote the Amalekites from Havilah until thou comest to Shur, that is over against Egypt. And he took Agag the king of the Amalekites alive, and utterly destroyed all the people with the edge of the sword. But Saul and the people spared Agag, and the best of the sheep, and of the oxen, and of the fatlings, and the lambs, and all that was good, and would not utterly destroy them: but every thing that was vile and refuse, that they destroyed utterly (I Samuel 15:7-9).

Saul actually filled the valley with dead men, women, children, cattle, camels, donkeys, sheep, everything they possessed. The Israelites killed them right and left, from one side of the country to the other. When it was all over the valley was full of death. Saul could say, "Look what I have done! Look at the thousands we have slain. I have slain the Amalekites!"

He came so close to obeying. He felt very sincere. He was not just playing the part of a hypocrite. His greeting to Samuel was, "Blessed be thou of the LORD: I have performed the commandment of the LORD" (I Samuel 15:13). Perhaps he was as sincere about what he had done as we are about our service today, but he did not obey *all* the Word of God through Samuel to him.

47

Saul's obedience was incomplete. His actions were not simply disobedience, but incomplete. He had been so near, so close, we can say ninety-nine percent complete. When there is ninety-nine percent obedience to enjoy, it is easy to overlook the one percent.

Saul tried to justify his action by blaming the people. "But the people took of the spoil, sheep and oxen, the chief of the things which should have been utterly destroyed, to sacrifice unto the LORD thy God in Gilgal" (I Samuel 15:21). Doesn't that sound so religious and so reasonable? It was hard for Saul to accept the blame.

Samuel had to let him know that to obey is better than to sacrifice. "And Samuel said, Hath the LORD as great delight in burnt offerings and sacrifice, as in obeying the voice of the LORD? Behold, to obey is better than sacrifice, and to hearken than the fat of rams" (I Samuel 15:22). There is no sacrifice to God that will substitute for obedience—not incomplete, but complete, obedience! Are we completely obedient to the Word of God?

Incomplete obedience is insufficient and unacceptable! Saul lived to rue the fact that it was his fault. No one else was to blame that he did not yield to God's will and comply with God's plan. He saw others take his place as time marched on, and God's order of things moved ahead.

It might prove good for us to get our eyes off the slain of the valley, and look in every nook and corner of the pasture where there may be a little lamb bleating or an ox lowing. Are we completely yielded to the Word of the living God, our Savior, our keeper, our healer, and our soon-coming king? If not, our incomplete obedience could have far-reaching effects for us as well as others.

Incomplete obedience cost Saul's posterity and cost

him his soul. "Then came the word of the LORD unto Samuel, saying, It repenteth me that I have set up Saul to be king: for he is turned back from following me, and hath not performed my commandments. . . . The LORD hath rent the kingdom of Israel from thee this day, and hath give it to a neighbour of thine, that is better than thou" (I Samuel 15:10-11, 28).

There is really no way to tell how far Saul's incomplete obedience reached into the future. Saul's family was established as the king's family. Jonathan was next in line for the throne. But the blessing of God was taken from Saul's household. The throne of Israel was given to another. Jonathan's descendants were never privileged to wear the crown. It wasn't too long until only *one* could be found who was connected with Saul's entire household.

After David became king he searched for and found Saul's grandson, the lame prince, Mephibosheth, living at Lodebar. David showed kindness to Mephibosheth for his friend Jonathan's sake, not Saul's sake. Incomplete obedience will affect more than just us. It affects the cause of God, and our posterity after us.

Saul was privileged to be chosen and used of God in His plan and design that reached back into the past and extended so far into the future. Though Saul failed and lost the reward, he did not alter God's economy. The Amalekites were later destroyed by another. (See I Samuel 27:8-9.)

Saul lived the life of a remorseful, driven man and finally died the death of suicide. (See I Samuel 31:4.) God let him run his course. He did not let lightning strike him, or let anyone kill him on the battlefield. If only he had taken time to consider what his incomplete obedience would cost him! This man slew thousands but reserved Agag and sheep and oxen against God's orders. It really cost him everything!

People like Saul, chosen of God, head and shoulders above the average, sometimes forsake the Lord. We should not be surprised when others forsake the ways of God. We need to mark the perfect man, even Jesus.

Saul's incomplete obedience affected God's eternal program. We are involved in the promise of God. The Old Testament saints are dependent upon us for perfection (completion). "And these all [Old Testament saints], having obtained a good report through faith, received not the promise: God having provided some better thing for us, that they without us should not be made perfect" (Hebrews 11:39-40). The saints of the Old Testament are dependent upon us, who have received the *promise* of the Holy Ghost, for the perfection of God's plan.

We can really see the far-reaching efforts of our incomplete obedience to the promise of God, not only for us personally, but for those dependent upon us for the completion of God's plan for them.

3

BACK TO BETHEL

Genesis 35:1

Outline

Introduction: Jacob gave this place its name, which means "the house of God," because God first met him there. God eventually called him back to Bethel, and to remember the vows he made to Him there.

I. Jacob's Ancestry and Life at Home
   A. He desires the birthright and blessing
      1. He buys the birthright from Esau
      2. He steals the blessing by deceit and Rebekah's help
   B. Esau—a warning example to faith professors (Hebrews 12:16)
   C. Esau threatens to kill Jacob

II. Jacob the Runaway
   A. His mother sends him to Haran
      1. To her brother Laban's house to seek a wife
      2. "I'll send for you when . . ."
   B. Jacob's first night of journey
      1. Jacob's dream—the ladder to heaven
      2. God spoke to Jacob in his dream
      3. Jacob's pillow of stone became an altar: "Bethel"
      4. Jacob's vow (Genesis 28:16-22)

III. Jacob Arrives in Harran and Meets Rachel at the Well

A. He goes home with Rachel and meets Laban, Rachel's father, his mother's brother
  1. He serves Laban seven years for Rachel
  2. By deceit, he is given Leah, then Rachel
     a. Jacob serves seven more years for Rachel
     b. Zilpah, Leah's handmaiden, and Bilhah, Rachel's handmaiden, also become wives of Jacob
     c. God blesses Jacob and Laban for Jacob's sake
     d. Jacob serves twenty years for all he obtained

IV. God Tells Jacob in a Dream to Return Home
  A. Jacob tells his family, and they prepare to leave
  B. The flight of Jacob
     1. Laban overtakes them
     2. God's message to Laban in a dream on how to treat Jacob
     3. Mizpah

V. Jacob Resumes His Journey toward Home
  A. Preparation to meet Esau: division of stock for a gift to Esau
  B. Jacob's prayer meeting in the night
     1. The wrestling match
     2. "What is thy name?"
     3. Jacob's confession
     4. Jacob, the "supplanter," becomes Israel, "prince with God"
  C. Jacob meets Esau
     1. His acceptance by Esau

2. Jacob stops at Shalem, a city of Shechem
3. Jacob worships in self-will and erects altar, El-elohe-Israel

VI. Jacob Reaps the Harvest of His Evil Years
   A. Shechem's defilement of Dinah
      1. Begs to be allowed to wed her
      2. Conditional consent given
      3. Deception by Simeon and Levi—slaying of Shechem's men
      4. Jacob is troubled

VII. God Calls Jacob to Go Back to Bethel
   A. Over thirty years lie between this call and his first meeting with God at Bethel
   B. Jacob's orders to his family
      1. Put away the strange gods among you
      2. Wash, be clean, change your garments
   C. Jacob erects another altar: El-Bethel, "The God of the House of God"

VIII. Back to Our Initial Experience
   A. The worth of a soul (Matthew 16:26)
   B. The day of preparation (II Corinthians 6:2)
      1. Lay aside idols
      2. Purity of heart: no malice, envy, strife, or jealousy
   C. The people in Acts received the Holy Ghost
      1. In Acts 4:31, they were refilled
      2. They spoke the Word of God boldly

BACK TO BETHEL

And Jacob awakened out of his sleep, and he said, Surely the LORD is in this place; and I knew it not. And he was afraid, and said, How dreadful is this place! this is none other but the house of God, and this is the gate of heaven. And Jacob rose up early in the morning, and took the stone that he had put for his pillows, and set it up for a pillar, and poured oil upon the top of it. And he called the name of that place Bethel: but the name of that city was called Luz at the first. And Jacob vowed a vow, saying, If God will be with me, and will keep me in this way that I go, and will give me bread to eat, and raiment to put on, so that I come again to my father's house in peace; then shall the LORD be my God: and this stone, which I have set for a pillar, shall be God's house: and of all thou shalt give me I will surely give the tenth unto thee (Genesis 28:16-22).

Jacob and Esau were twin sons born to Isaac and Rebekah. The birthright and blessing belonged to the firstborn, Esau. Jacob coveted, and wanted more than anything else in all the world, the birthright and blessing. He schemed until he obtained both. The sale of the birthright came about as told in Genesis 25:27-34:

And the boys grew: and Esau was a cunning hunter, a man of the field; and Jacob was a plain man, dwelling in tents. And Isaac loved Esau, because he did eat of his venison: but Rebekah loved Jacob. And Jacob sod pottage: and Esau came from the field, and he was faint: and Esau said to Jacob, Feed me, I pray thee, with that same red

57

pottage; for I am faint: therefore was his name called Edom. And Jacob said, Sell me this day thy birthright. And Esau said, Behold, I am at the point to die: and what profit shall this birthright do to me? And Jacob said, Swear to me this day; and he sware unto him: and he sold his birthright unto Jacob. Then Jacob gave Esau bread and pottage of lentils; and he did eat and drink, and rose up, and went his way: thus Esau despised his birthright.

Esau typifies a carnal man (Hebrews 12:16). In many ways he was a more noble man than Jacob, but he had no faith. He despised the birthright because it was a spiritual thing of no value to him. He had no faith to conceive of its value and the promises accompanying it.

The birthright included at least three spiritual benefits. First, the eldest son became the head of the family and as such exercised priestly rights, until the Aaronic priesthood was established. Second, the descendants of Abraham held the Edenic promise of Genesis 3:15: out of them would come the bruiser of Satan's head. Third, they were inheritors of the promise of Genesis 12:3: through them the whole world would be blessed.

Esau sold all these rights for a moment's fleshly gratification. Jacob's idea of the birthright was defective, carnal, and inadequate, but his desire for it showed true faith.

Hebrews 12:16-17 uses Esau to issue a warning to those who merely profess faith, less they miss the spiritual priesthood: "Lest there be any fornicator, or profane person, as Esau, who for one morsel of meat sold his birthright. For ye know how that afterward, when he would have inherited the blessing, he was rejected: for he found no place of repentance, though he sought it carefully with tears."

We could say Jacob *bought* the birthright, and he schemed until he *stole* the blessing.

And it came to pass, that when Isaac was old, and his eyes were dim, so that he could not see, he called Esau his eldest son, and said unto him, My son: and he said unto him, Behold, here am I. And he said, Behold now, I am old, I know not the day of my death: now therefore take, I pray thee, thy weapons, thy quiver and thy bow, and go out to the field, and take me some venison; and make me savoury meat, such as I love, and bring it to me, that I may eat; that my soul may bless thee before I die. And Rebekah heard when Isaac spake to Esau his son. And Esau went to the field to hunt for venison, and to bring it (Genesis 27:1-5).

Jacob wanted that blessing! His mother was with him; she wanted him to have it! She told Jacob about the conversation of Isaac and Esau that she had overheard. Then she told him what to do. "Fetch me two good kids of the goats. I will make savory meat for your father. I'll disguise you, and you serve him. He will bless you, thinking that he is blessing Esau." (Isaac's eyesight was so bad that he could hardly see.)

Rebekah took Esau's clothes for Jacob to dress in. She put the skins from the kids upon his hands and the back of his neck. Jacob asked Rebekah, "What if my father discovers me? I will seem to him as a deceiver, and bring a curse upon me, and not a blessing."

His mother answered, "Upon me be your curse, my son."

59

Jacob took the prepared dish and bread to Isaac and said, "My father."

Isaac asked, "Who are you, my son?"

"I am Esau, your firstborn," Jacob answered. "I have done as you bade me. Sit and eat of my venison, that your soul may bless me."

Isaac conversed with Jacob and said, "Come near that I may feel you, to see whether you are my son Esau or not." Jacob went near his father; he felt him and said, "The voice is Jacob's, but the hands are the hands of Esau. Are you truly my son Esau?"

Jacob responded, "I am."

Isaac then said, "Bring the food to me. I will eat of my son's venison, that my soul may bless you." After that he ate and drank.

Then Isaac said unto him, "Come near and kiss me, my son." When Jacob did so, Isaac smelled his clothing and blessed him, saying, "See, the smell of my son is as the smell of a field which the LORD hath blessed: therefore God give thee of the dew of heaven, and the fatness of the earth, and plenty of corn and wine: let people serve thee, and nations bow down to thee: be lord over thy brethren, and let thy mother's sons bow down to thee: cursed be every one that curseth thee, and blessed be he that blesseth thee" (Genesis 27:27-29).

Isaac gave Jacob the blessing that belonged to Esau. Jacob was scarcely out of the house when Esau came in with the venison he had prepared. When Isaac realized what he had done in blessing Jacob, he trembled greatly. Esau remarked that Jacob, whose name meant supplanter, was rightly named. "He is a cheat, a defrauder. He cheated me out of my birthright; now he has stolen my blessing."

Esau purposed in his heart to kill Jacob. He decided, It won't be long until my father dies. After the days of mourning are over I am going to kill Jacob.

When Rebekah heard of this she called Jacob to her and said, "I want you to go to Haran, to my father Laban's house. When Esau's anger is dim I will send for you."

She told Isaac, "I don't want Jacob marrying one of the girls here in this land. If Jacob marries one of the daughters of Heth, what good shall my life do me?"

The thought was planted. Her scheme worked. Isaac sent for Jacob and told him to go to his mother's people in Padan-aram, in the land of Haran, and take a wife of Laban's daughters. Jacob actually went to escape the wrath of Esau!

It was several days' journey to Haran. When night came, Jacob prepared to sleep on the ground. He took some stones and made a pillow. In his sleep God showed him a ladder reaching from heaven to earth, with angels ascending and descending, and the Lord stood at the top of the ladder.

The Lord talked to Jacob and told him to go on to Haran, that He would be with him and bless him. Jacob said to the Lord, "If You will go with me, bless me, give me food and clothing, and bring me back in peace and safety to my father's house, I will surely give the tenth to You." He did not merely say *a* tenth. Tithing had already been a practice, so he said *the* tenth.

The next morning he took his pillow of stone and set it up for a pillar, anointed the pillar with oil, and named the place Bethel, meaning "the house of God." Then he went on his way to Haran.

Arriving in Haran, he went to a well where the women came to draw water. He was not there long until Rachel came along. He told Rachel who he was. Finding that Rachel's father, Laban, was his mother's brother, he went home with her. Laban took Jacob in. After a month passed, Laban told him, "It isn't fair that you labor for me for nothing. What shall your wages be?"

Jacob replied, "I'll work for you seven years if you will give me Rachel, your younger daughter."

Laban said, "It is better that I give her to you than to another man."

"Jacob served seven years for Rachel; and they seemed unto him but a few days, for the love he had to her" (Genesis 29:20).

The day of the wedding came. Imagine Jacob's surprise the next morning when he found that he had married Leah instead of Rachel. The Oriental custom of heavy veiling had concealed the identity of Leah at the wedding.

The resulting confrontation between Jacob and Laban is found in Genesis 29:27-28. Jacob told Laban, "You have deceived me! You promised that if I worked for you seven years, you would give me Rachel. You tricked me and gave Leah to me instead!"

Laban answered him, "It is against the custom of my country that the younger daughter be given before the firstborn. If you will work for me seven more years you may have Rachel also. Stay with Leah this week and you may take Rachel to wife."

Jacob was beginning to reap what he had sown! Did he think of how he had cheated and robbed Esau? As a man sows, so shall he reap. This is an inevitable law of God. (See Galatians 6:7-8.)

Laban gave Zilpah as a maid to Leah, and to Rachel he gave Bilhah as her maid.

Jacob loved Rachel more than Leah, and he served seven more years. To Rachel, Leah, and their maids were born the sons of Jacob.

Through the years God blessed the households of both Jacob and Laban because of Jacob. Eleven sons were born to Jacob while in Haran; only Benjamin was born after his departure. Then God spoke to Jacob in a dream, "I am the God of Bethel, where thou anointedst the pillar, and where thou vowedst a vow unto me: now arise, get thee out from this land, and return unto the land of thy kindred" (Genesis 31:13).

No doubt Jacob wondered, Back to my father's house? And Esau? Yes, Jacob, you cannot run from life! God is good to call you to face past deeds, and give an account while in this present world.

Then Jacob rose up, and set his sons and his wives upon camels; and he carried away all his cattle, and all his goods which he had gotten, the cattle of his getting, which he had gotten in Padan-aram, for to go to Isaac his father in the land of Canaan. And Laban went to shear his sheep: and Rachel had stolen the images that were her father's. And Jacob stole away unawares to Laban the Syrian, in that he told him not that he fled. So he fled with all that he had; and he rose up, and passed over the river, and set his face toward the mount Gilead. And it was told Laban on the third day that Jacob was fled. And he took his brethren with him, and pursued after him seven days' journey, and they overtook him in the mount Gilead. And God came to Laban the Syrian in a dream by night, and

63

said unto him, Take heed that thou speak not to Jacob either good or bad (Genesis 31:17-24).

Laban chided Jacob for secretly fleeing away with his daughters and their children. "If you so longed for your father's house, why didn't you say so? I could have sent you away with mirth, with songs, with tabret, and with harp. If you so wanted to go, why have you stolen my gods?"

Jacob gave Laban an honest answer: "Because I was afraid! Afraid you would take by force your daughters from me! As for your gods, whoever you find them with, let him not live." (Jacob did not know that Rachel had stolen the images.)

Jacob was angry! "What is my trespass? What is my sin? You have searched and not found one thing I have taken. I have been twenty-six years in your house. I served fourteen years for your daughters, six years for your cattle, and you changed my wages ten times. Except God had been with me, you would have sent me away empty. God has seen my affliction, the labor of my hands, and rebuked you last night."

Laban answered, "What can I do to my daughters and children? They are mine, too. Let us make a covenant. Let it be for a witness between me and you."

Jacob ordered his relatives to gather stones and make a heap for a witness, and they ate upon it. Laban told Jacob, "The LORD watch between me and thee, when we are absent one from another." Laban rose up early in the morning, kissed his sons and daughters, blessed them, and departed to his place.

As Jacob went on his way, the angels of God met him.

When he saw them he said, "This is God's host." He named the place Mahanaim, which means *two* hosts, or bands. Not only was there the visible band of Jacob and his servants, but there was also the invisible band of God's angels.

This visitation must have reassured Jacob. He sent messengers before him to Esau, instructing them to tell him: "Thy servant Jacob saith thus, I have sojourned with Laban, and stayed there until now: and I have oxen, and asses, flocks, and menservants, and womenservants: and I have sent to tell my lord, that I may find grace in thy sight" (Genesis 32:4-5).

The messengers returned to Jacob saying, "We came to thy brother Esau, and also he cometh to meet thee, and four hundred men with him" (Genesis 32:6).

Then Jacob was greatly afraid and distressed. He divided the people and animals and everything he had into two bands, saying, "If Esau smites one company, then the other shall escape." Then Jacob prayed! He really prayed. "O God of my father Abraham, and God of my father Isaac, You told me to return to my kindred, and You would deal well with me. I know I'm not worthy of the least of all Your mercies, and of all the truth that You have shown to Your servant. I passed over Jordan with only my staff; now I am two bands! Deliver me, I pray, from my brother, Esau: for I fear him, lest he will come and smite me, and the mother with the children. You said You would surely do me good, and make my seed as the sand of the sea, which cannot be numbered."

Jacob's prayer shows that much of the old Jacob was gone! He had left a lot of selfishness behind. His prayer told God that he was looking to and counting on God to

65

get him out of the web he had woven years before.

The Lord must have led him and shown him what to do. Jacob prepared the following present, a "peace offering," for his brother: two hundred she-goats, twenty he-goats, two hundred ewes, twenty rams, thirty milk camels with their colts, forty cows, ten bulls, twenty she-donkeys, and ten colts. He placed them into the charge of his servants, every drove by itself, and said to his servants, "Pass over before me and put a space between each drove. When you meet my brother, Esau, and he asks, 'Whose are you? Where are you going? And whose are these animals before you?' then you shall say, 'They are your servant Jacob's; it is a present sent to my lord Esau. He is coming behind us.'"

So went the presents over before him, and Jacob lodged there that night. He arose in the night, took his two wives, his two maids, and his eleven sons, and sent them with everything he had over the brook Jabbok, and Jacob was left alone.

Jacob was left alone! There are times of pressure and loneliness, even in a crowd, when we feel we must get alone with God. Only He can sustain and undergird us. We do what we can, as God leads, and then we must leave the matter with Him.

Jacob felt the need to be alone with his friend, his God, in prayer. The result is found in Genesis 32:24-31:

And Jacob was left alone; and there wrestled a man with him until the breaking of the day. And when he saw that he prevailed not against him, he touched the hollow of his thigh; and the hollow of Jacob's thigh was out of joint, as he wrestled with him. And he said, Let me go, for the day breaketh. And he said, I will not let thee go, except thou bless me. And he said unto him, What is thy name? . . .

This was Jacob's crisis, the crisis of his life!

Now Jacob was face to face with his past. He had touched God! He decided, "I won't let go unless You forgive me. I must know that You have. I am completely helpless, Lord God. Only You can give me what I need!"

And he said, Jacob.

He let go of everything when he confessed his name: "I am Jacob. I have lied, I have cheated, I am a thief, I am a supplanter!" There it was: all laid out before God.

And he said, Thy name shall be called no more Jacob, but Israel: for as a prince hast thou power with God and with men, and have prevailed.

Oh, sweet balm of Gilead! How soothing to the soul!

How long the communion between Jacob and his God was, we do not know. We can only read between the lines of "What is thy name?" Suddenly Jacob asked a question in turn.

And Jacob asked him, and said, Tell me, I pray thee, thy name.

How many patriarchs and prophets of old asked that question? How many writers inquired for God's name?

What a blessed people we are! In only a moment, we

can breathe the name of Jesus! That is the name in which we have been granted repentance, baptism, and the infilling of the Holy Spirit, the name after which the whole family of God, both in heaven and in earth, is named.

> *And he said, Wherefore is it that thou dost ask after my name? And he blessed him there. And Jacob called the name of the place Peniel [The face of God]: for I have seen God face to face, and my life is preserved. And as he passed over Penuel the sun rose upon him, and he halted upon his thigh.*

Only after he was touched by God was Jacob's name changed to Israel. Both names are applied to the nation descended from Jacob.

Jacob is the name for the natural posterity of Abraham, Isaac, and Jacob. Israel is the name for the spiritual nation. The promises of God were given to all the people, to "Jacob"; but only those who were spiritual, "Israel," comprehended and received them.

God chose Israel for a fourfold mission:

1. To witness to the oneness of God in the midst of universal idolatry (Deuteronomy 6:4; Isaiah 43:10-12).
2. To show nations the blessedness of serving the true God (Deuteronomy 33:26-29; I Chronicles 17:20-21; Psalm 144:15).
3. To receive, preserve, and transmit the Scriptures (Deuteronomy 4:5-8; Romans 3:1-2).
4. To produce, as to his humanity, the Messiah (Genesis 3:15; 12:3; 22:18; 28:10-14; 49:10; II Samuel 7:12-16; Isaiah 7:14; 9:6; Matthew 1:1; Romans 1:3).

Jacob saw Esau coming with four hundred men. Jacob divided the children among Leah, Rachel, and the two maids. He put the maids and their children first, Leah and her children next, and Rachel and Joseph last. He passed by them and bowed himself to the ground seven times until he came near to his brother.

At last they met! They had to bridge a span of over thirty years, plus Jacob's actions at home before he left. Jacob had done his homework for his meeting, and God did not fail him.

Esau ran to meet him, embraced him, fell on his neck, kissed him, and they wept. "Who are all these with you?" Esau inquired. It seems that Esau was somewhat astonished at all his eyes saw.

"They are children God has graciously given your servant," Jacob replied. He introduced his family as each mother with her children came before Esau and bowed before him.

"What do you mean by all the drove I met?" Esau wanted to know.

"These are to find grace in the sight of my lord," replied Jacob.

"I have enough my brother; keep what you have for yourself," Esau said.

But Jacob insisted, "Please, take my blessing I brought you. God has dealt graciously with me. I have enough." Finally, Esau agreed to take it.

"Let us go home," Esau urged Jacob.

"Please let my lord pass over before his servant. I will lead on softly, according as the cattle and the children are able to endure, until I come to my lord unto Seir," pleaded Jacob.

Quite a change was noticeable in Jacob. An encounter with God changes all. But "Jacob" does not cease to dominate the walk of "Israel" all at once. The wrestling match did not quite put everything in order, as we shall see a little later, when his walk finally conformed to his new name.

Jacob resumed his travel. He stopped at a certain place, built a house, made booths for the cattle, and named the place Succoth, meaning booths.

Later Jacob came to Shalem, a city of Shechem in Canaan. From Hamor, the ruler of the country, he bought the field. He erected there an altar; Jacob worshiped in self-will. He named the altar El-elohe-Israel, that is, "God, the God of Israel."

Jacob reaped the harvest of his evil years while at the city of Shechem. It came about in this manner: Leah's daughter, Dinah, went visiting with the daughters of the land. Shechem, son of Hamor, saw Dinah, took her, and defiled her. He fell in love with her and begged his father to let him marry her.

Jacob heard of Shechem's defilement of Dinah. His sons were in the field with the cattle. Jacob held his peace until they came home. The men were grieved and very angry.

Shechem pleaded with Dinah's father and brothers: "Let me find grace in your eyes. Ask me ever so much dowry. I will give as you ask. Only give me Dinah to wife."

The sons of Jacob answered Hamor and Shechem deceitfully, "We will consent if every male of you will be circumcised as we are."

Hamor conferred with the men of his city. They complied with the request.

On the third day when all the men were convalescing, two sons of Jacob, Simeon and Levi, took a sword, came boldly upon the city, slew all the males, took Dinah out of Shechem's house, and took possession of everything.

Jacob was troubled and told his sons, "You have made me to stink among the inhabitants of this land. We are few in number. They will slay us. Our house will be destroyed."

And God said unto Jacob, Arise, go up to Bethel, and dwell there: and make there an altar unto God, that appeared unto thee when thou fleddest from the face of Esau thy brother. Then Jacob said unto his household, and to all that were with him, Put away the strange gods that are among you, and be clean, and change your garments: and let us arise, and go up to Bethel; and I will make there an altar unto God, who answered me in the day of my distress, and was with me in the way which I went. And they gave unto Jacob all the strange gods which were in their hand, and all their earrings which were in their ears; and Jacob hid them under the oak which was by Shechem. . . . So Jacob came to Luz, which is in the land of Canaan, that is, Bethel, he and all the people that were with him. And he built there an altar, and called the place El-beth-el (Genesis 35:1-7).

There is a sermon with an exhortation in almost every line of the foregoing passage of Scriptures. For the present let us consider: "Arise, and go up to Bethel."

What did it mean for Jacob to go back to Bethel? Bethel was the house of God, the place where Jacob first met God. It was his first encounter with God, where he first talked to Him, where he made his first vows, his first experience with God! It was time to pay his vows.

Before we go on with Jacob let us remember: we should all go back to our first encounter and renew our initial experience with God, where He accepted us and we made our vows to Him, and, yes, "pray through" again.

One man said, "I don't believe in going back." He probably needed to go back more than anyone else. The people in the second chapter of Acts received the Holy Ghost, and in the fourth chapter the same people were filled with the Holy Ghost again: "And when they had prayed, the place was shaken where they were assembled together; and they were all filled with the Holy Ghost, and they spake the word of God with boldness" (Acts 4:31).

There were *thirty years* between Bethel and where Jacob was now! It makes no difference how many years there are between us and our first encounter with God. He is waiting! We can renew our vows, our consecration, anytime we go back to Him! His arms are open to us!

Every minister and every teacher lives with and longs to create a desire in every heart for a renewal, a refilling in the Holy Ghost for you just as you first received.

Jacob spoke with his family about what God had told him to do. He began to make special arrangements and changes for going back to Bethel. One of the first things they did was get rid of their idol gods they brought from Haran. (Rachel had stolen her father's.) They also took off their jewelry. Jacob hid these things under the oak of Shechem.

What would God require of us if we purposed in our heart that we were going back to our initial experience with Him? We should not have to give up anything. We should have kept ourselves as clean and pure as when we first committed ourselves to Him. If there are things we once gave up and have returned to, those things may keep us out of the Rapture, and out of heaven.

Every country has its idol gods. America is filled with them. As we read the Old Testament we notice that on several occasions the Israelites had to spend some time in prayer, seeking God, putting aside their idols, and making another consecration to God.

Amos 4:12 says, "Prepare to meet thy God." He has given us a day of preparation. About ninety percent of our preparation in the church today is not to meet God. It is preparing to teach a class, preparing to preach a sermon, checking and preparing to visit absentees to keep them in, preparing our classrooms, and many other things. All of this is necessary, but sometimes preparing to meet God seems to be altogether out of the question, beside the point. "What is a man profited, if he shall gain the whole world, and lose his own soul? or what shall a man give in exchange for his soul?" (Matthew 16:26). We *are* going to meet Jesus.

If you are not prepared, take time now. "Behold, now is the accepted time; behold, now is the day of salvation" (II Corinthians 6:2).

Jacob knew exactly what God meant when he said, "Go up to Bethel." He remembered his initial encounter with God, even though it was more than thirty years before, where he saw a ladder reaching from heaven to earth, angels ascending and descending, with the Lord

73

standing at the top of the ladder in heaven. Jacob had exclaimed, "This is the gate to heaven! The Lord is in this place!" We know beyond a shadow of doubt when we find ourselves in the gate of heaven. We should keep our gate to heaven and to God open at all times.

Jacob remembered setting up a pillar and anointing it with oil. He knew he was in touch with God, and he made some vows. It was such a precious, special time with God; the memory was not dim. It was yet alive to Jacob, so alive he was ready to go up.

We know when the Spirit is drawing us. If this is not true in your life, obey James 4:8: "Draw nigh to God, and he will draw nigh to you."

For over thirty years Jacob knew he had to make things right with his brother before things were right with him and God. Could this be a reason for many people not praying through? Not one of us received the Holy Ghost while harboring one ounce of malice in our heart. We can pray until we are hoarse, but until we make things right with others we will not be able to touch Him.

Jacob struggled, wrestling in prayer into the early morning hours. No doubt he became weak and tired. God told him, "Let me go; day is breaking." God did not have to say that. Was God testing Jacob? Would any of us have let go? God could have let go and disengaged himself at any time. Of course He could! But He would not do it then, and He will not do it now if we are as determined as Jacob: "I won't let you go unless you bless me."

The apostle Paul said, "As ye have therefore received Christ Jesus the Lord, so walk ye in him" (Colossians 2:6).

It is interesting to observe the progressive steps of Jacob with God as God directed him, until he reached the

74

level of maturity in worship that God desires for each of us. First, Jacob, the runaway, was on his way to Haran when he encountered God at Bethel, "The House of God." Next, as Jacob was on the way home after the wrestling match, he worshiped in self-will at an altar he erected on his own and named El-elohe-Israel, "God the God of Israel." Finally, God called Jacob back to Bethel. It then became El-beth-el, "The God of the house of God."

4

SATAN AMONG THE SAINTS
Job 1:6-12

Outline

Introduction: If Satan would place himself among the servants of God back during Job's day, it is reasonable to believe that he will today.

I. Satan's Purpose
   A. It is for no good cause
   B. It is not to worship God
   C. To place a deceitful, withholding attitude in us
   D. To accuse the brethren
   E. To encourage disobedience
      His purpose in the garden (Genesis 3:4-5)
   F. To steal away the Word from hearers lest they believe (Luke 8:12)

II. His Works among the Saints
   A. The first church at Jerusalem
      1. Ananias and Sapphira (Acts 5:1-11)
      2. He encouraged Ananias and Sapphira to hold back
      3. He still causes people to hold back
   B. Among the chosen disciples
      1. Satan entered into Judas (Luke 22:1-4)
   C. The chosen disciple, Peter (Matthew 16:21-24)

III. To Hinder the Service of God

SATAN AMONG THE SAINTS

Now there was a day when the sons of God came to present themselves before the LORD, and Satan came also among them. And the LORD said unto Satan, Whence comest thou? Then Satan answered the LORD, and said, From going to and fro in the earth, and from walking up and down in it. And the LORD said unto Satan, Hast thou considered my servant Job, that there is none like him in the earth, a perfect and an upright man, one that feareth God, and escheweth evil? Then Satan answered the LORD, and said, Doth Job fear God for nought? Hast not thou made an hedge about him, and about his house, and about all that he hath on every side? thou hast blessed the work of his hands, and his substance is increased in the land. But put forth thine hand now, and touch all that he hath, and he will curse thee to thy face. And the LORD said unto Satan, Behold, all that he hath is in thy power; only upon himself put not forth thine hand. So Satan went forth from the presence of the LORD (Job 1:6-12).

Satan among the saints! Notice that I did not say Satan *in* the saints, but Satan *among* the saints.

There was a certain day during the time of Job when the sons of God came to present themselves before the Lord. That is what we do when we go to church: present ourselves to the Lord. Satan mingled among them and also came along. The Scriptures let us know that in the past it was possible for Satan to assemble with the children of God, and it is still possible today! Is it hard to accept that Satan dares to invade our sacred sanctuaries to sit among the saints? If he placed himself among the sons of God in Job's day, it is not hard to accept that he will visit in our congregations!

The Scripture does not tell us where the sons of God came together. It does say they came to present themselves before the Lord. They came together to honor and serve God and to acknowledge His supremacy.

When we understand Satan's purpose for visiting our assemblies, it will not seem so surprising after all. Let us examine his reasons for attending church.

Oh yes, he does go to church! Many ministers will attest to that fact. Saints will also say that he does. Why does he go? *He does not go for any good reason!*

First of all, he will try to keep you from going if he can. That is a strange thing about Satan. He will do everything he can to keep you away, but even if he is successful he will go anyway! If he cannot keep you from going he will come along with you. He will walk right in and sit down with you.

Please do not take him along with you. You can do so by going to church against your will, saying or thinking, "I have no business going to church tonight. I just don't feel well, and I need to finish up that little job I started." If you feel like finishing up the little job, you feel well enough to go to church. If you do go in that frame of mind, Satan will be so pleased to accompany you. You will be in the right mood to find fault with everything. Nothing will be right. Satan will help you feed the old carnal nature, while the spiritual man goes hungry.

Why does Satan attend church? He does not go for any good reason. *He does not worship God!* That is the last thought on his mind. He can be in an assembly with no thought of worshiping, none whatsoever. And he will keep us from worshiping if he can! Our purpose for attending is to present ourselves before the Lord and to exalt Him in worship. Satan will not sing one song, lift his hands in praise, offer one handclap, or worship in the Spirit. Never would he offer an amen to support the pastor.

The name of Lucifer means "light bearer" and "daystar." Lucifer was at one time an archangel in heaven. Ezekiel 28:12-15 describes the unfallen state of Lucifer, who became Satan:

Thou sealest up the sum, full of wisdom, and perfect in beauty. Thou hast been in Eden the garden of God; every precious stone was thy covering, the sardius, topaz, and the diamond, the beryl, the onyx, and the jasper, the sapphire, the emerald, and the carbuncle, and gold: the workmanship of thy tabrets and of thy pipes was prepared in thee in the day that thou was created. Thou art the anointed cherub that covereth; and I have set thee so: thou wast upon the holy mountain of God; thou hast walked up and down in the midst of the stones of fire. Thou wast perfect in thy ways from the day that thou wast created, till iniquity was found in thee.

But then he fell. Jesus told His disciples, "I beheld Satan as lightning fall from heaven" (Luke 10:18). In Isaiah 14:12-14 we read of his expulsion from heaven:

How art thou fallen from heaven, O Lucifer, son of the morning! How are thou cut down to the ground, which didst weaken the nations! For thou hast said in thine heart, I will ascend into heaven, I will exalt my throne above the

stars of God: I will sit also upon the mount of the congrega-
tion, in the sides of the north: I will ascend above the heights
of the clouds; I will be like the most High.

This passage marks the beginning of sin in the
universe. When Lucifer said, "I will," sin began.

From his decription in Ezekiel we find he has wisdom.
From Isaiah we find his purpose for assembling with the
people of God: He really would like to take over the service. Many times that is why the pulpit has to battle
against him.

Let me show you what he did in the early church, the
First Church of Jerusalem. If he can get by with it, he
will do the same in our church today. He did not do his
evil deed in some back alley. He did not do it on the other
side of the tracks or in the sinful area of the city. He did
it among the saints of the early church. In Acts 4:32-35
we read:

And the multitude of them that believed were of one
heart and one soul: neither said any of them that ought
of the things which he possessed was his own; but they had
all things common. And with great power gave the apostles
witness of the resurrection of the Lord Jesus: and great
grace was upon them all. Neither was there any among
them that lacked: for as many as were possessors of lands
or houses sold them, and brought the prices of the things
that were sold, and laid them down at the apostles' feet,
and distribution was made unto every man according as
he had need.

It was because of their overwhelming love and thanksgiving toward Jesus and for one another that the believers were moved to do this. Even so, I imagine there was a grumbler or two who said one to the other, "That's too much money for those preachers to handle."

There was one couple who turned out to be hypocrites. In Acts 5:1-11 we have the account:

But a certain man named Ananias, with Sapphira his wife, sold a possession, and kept back part of the price, his wife also being privy to it, and brought a certain part, and laid it at the apostles' feet. But Peter said, Ananias, why hath Satan filled thine heart to lie to the Holy Ghost, and to keep back part of the price of the land? Whiles it remained, was it not thine own? and after it was sold, was it not in thine own power? why hast thou conceived this thing in thine heart? thou hast not lied unto men, but unto God. And Ananias hearing these words fell down, and gave up the ghost: and great fear came on all them that heard these things. And the young men arose, wound him up, and carried him out, and buried him. And it was about the space of three hours after, when his wife, not knowing what was done, came in. And Peter answered unto her, Tell me whether ye sold the land for so much? And she said, Yea, for so much. Then Peter said unto her, How is it that ye have agreed together to tempt the Spirit of the Lord? behold, the feet of them which have buried thy husband are at the door, and shall carry thee out. Then fell she down straightway at his feet, and yielded up the ghost: and the young men came in, and found her dead, and carrying her forth, buried her by her husband. And great fear came upon all the church, and upon as many as heard these things.

Peter rebuked Ananias by asking, "Why have you allowed Satan to put it into your heart to lie to the Holy Ghost?" Just as it happened back then, Satan would like to do the same in our congregations today. He would like *to put a deceitful, withholding attitude in your heart.* Not only does he want you to hold back part of your tithe and offering, but he will encourage you to withhold yourself from the service. Of course, he cannot unless you are willing. Instead of your worshiping God when the assembly sings "Victory in Jesus," he will encourage you not to sing. He does not want you to enjoy victory. He also knows that your participation might help someone else as well.

The Scripture says that God inhabits the praises of Israel. Satan does not want you to praise the Lord. If he can hinder you, he will. When we praise the Lord, we entertain God's Spirit into our midst. What better way could we overcome unwelcome spirits than to praise God?

Job was one of the most righteous men who ever lived. God said so, and God knows! He asked Satan, "Have you taken a look at Job's life?" Could the Lord bring our life to the attention of the enemy? God stated further to Satan, "There is no one like Job! He is perfect. He is upright. He has reverence for God. He shuns the very appearance of evil."

I imagine Satan scratched his head and was at a loss for words until he thought and sneeringly said, "Oh, yeah? Job has his reasons for serving You. He does not fear You for nothing. You have not only put a hedge around him, but about all that he has. You have blessed his work and increased all his substance. You have made him a rich man. Job knows what he is doing. Just take away the hedges. He will curse you to your face."

Why does Satan assemble with the children of God? Here is another reason: *he is an accuser of the brethren!* (See Revelation 12:10.)

God was not afraid to put Job to the test of Satan. Can He allow one of us to be tested? If it were necessary God could! He has always had a people. He has more to-day than ever before. That is reasonable to assume, for there are more people today. We have been busy getting the gospel to people, and more are recipients of salvation.

Notice the wisdom of God. He asked, "Hast thou considered my servant Job?" That was, and is, a wise move. In the vernacular of today we would say, "God beat Satan to the draw!" Before Satan could bring up some hypocritical person, God placed Job before him.

When we read about Job, we understand that he was a unique person, a man of character. He was an outstanding person of influence. Job was the greatest man of his day in the society to which he belonged. He was the finest, strongest, most complete man of integrity to be found. He was the best and purest chosen by God to represent humanity in a contest of the ages, on the battleground of the soul! Job's character is summed up in God's statement: "There is none like him, a perfect and an upright man, and one that feared God, and eschewed evil." It is no wonder that God focused Satan's attention on Job! God knew His man!

We must remember: Satan is an accuser! He hates all noble-mindedness, all that is pure and lofty, all that God imparts to mankind. He seeks to destroy the spiritual.

When God asked, "Whence comest thou?" Satan answered, "From going to and fro in the earth, and from walking up and down in it." The earth is his hunting ground. He is never still, but ever restless, seeking to destroy. We can see Satan among the saints.

The attack of Satan soon came upon Job's life. (See Job 1:14-19.) A messenger came to tell Job, "The oxen were plowing, and the asses feeding beside them: and the Sabeans fell upon them, and took them away; yea, they have slain the servants with the edge of the sword; and I only am escaped to tell thee." Another messenger came and said, "The fire of God is fallen from heaven and hath burned up the sheep, and the servants, and consumed them; and I only am escaped alone to tell thee." A third messenger came with the news, "The Chaldeans . . . fell upon the camels, and have carried them away, yea, and slain the servants with the edge of the sword; and I only am escaped alone to tell thee." A fourth messenger brought the news, "Thy sons and thy daughters were eating and drinking in their eldest brother's house: and, behold, there came a great wind from the wilderness, and smote the four corners of the house, and it fell upon the young men, and they are dead; and I only am escaped alone to tell thee."

What would you have done had this befallen you?

Job stood stripped of possessions, destitute, childless, without property, almost homeless. His whole environment had changed.

How did he react? Job proved that what was in him was greater than the external. He proved that circumstances are only temporary arrangements. This man was not what he had, but he was what he was.

Job arose, tore his mantle, shaved his head, fell upon the ground, and worshiped, saying, "Naked came I out of my mother's womb, and naked shall I return thither: the LORD gave, and the LORD hath taken away; blessed be the name of the LORD" (Job 1:21).

"In all this Job sinned not, nor charged God foolishly" (Job 1:22).

Satan is among the saints, an accuser of the brethren. Don't ever forget: "the devil, as a roaring lion, walketh about, seeking whom he may devour" (I Peter 5:8).

Satan is attending to his business! He will always try to get at you. Be aware of his tactics, and you will not be susceptible to them.

There are three votes, only three, to be cast for your soul. Jesus voted so strongly for your soul that He became your sacrifice for sin. Satan casts one vote against you. Now the vote is tied! *You* hold the deciding ballot.

Satan also likes to be among the saints *to encourage disobedience!* Let us visit the Garden of Eden and notice what the Scriptures say:

And the LORD God planted a garden eastward in Eden; and there he put the man whom he had formed. And out of the ground made the LORD God to grow every tree that is pleasant to the sight, and good for food; the tree of life also in the midst of the garden, and the tree of knowledge of good and evil. And a river went out of Eden to water the garden. . . . And the LORD God took the man, and put him into the garden of Eden to dress it and to keep it (Genesis 2:8-10, 15).

The Garden of Eden was one of the most beautiful places ever created. It was a godly paradise, created for the good of man. Adam and Eve were blessed of God to have such a place to live and commune with their Creator. He gave them everything they needed in that beautiful setting. The birds of the air flying about from tree to tree, filling the air with their singing, made it even more peaceful and serene.

Why did Satan visit the Garden of Eden? Genesis 3 shows that he came to encourage disobedience. "Now the serpent was more subtil than any beast of the field which the LORD God had made. And he said unto the woman, Yea, hath God said, ye shall not eat of every tree of the garden?" (Genesis 3:1).

Let us notice how subtle the enemy is. With that one question he planted in Eve's mind a doubt about the goodness and benevolence of God. There were many trees with all different kinds of fruits to choose from. Everything they needed was there. But Satan knew how to pose his question to take Eve's mind off everything but that one tree! When he asked that question she momentarily forgot everything else in the garden. In a flash her mind went to that one tree! "And the woman said unto the serpent, We may eat of the fruit of the trees of the garden: But of the fruit of the tree which is in the midst of the garden, God hath said, Ye shall not eat of it, neither shall ye touch it, lest ye die" (Genesis 3:2-3).

Now let us listen to the enemy add to the Word of God and lie. "And the serpent said unto the woman, Ye shall not surely die: for God doth know that in the day ye eat thereof, then your eyes shall be opened, and ye shall be as gods, knowing good and evil" (Genesis 3:5). The enemy slyly insinuated that Eve was walking around in a stupor, unaware that God was holding back something good from her. Doubt was again raised. Satan's temptation of Eve appealed to her pride.

Ezekiel 28:15 says of Lucifer, "Thou was perfect in thy ways from the day that thou was created, till iniquity was found in thee." In Isaiah 14:12-14 he said, "I will" five times:

- "I will ascend into heaven"
- "I will exalt my throne above the stars of God"
- "I will sit also upon the mount of the congregation"
- "I will ascend above the heights of the clouds"
- "I will be like the most High"

Pride was the iniquity found in Lucifer. Now he tempted Eve through pride. He used the very same thing on her that brought about his downfall and expulsion from heaven. Poor Eve. She fell for it. "And when the woman saw that the tree was good for food, and that it was pleasant to the eyes, and a tree to be desired to make one wise, she took of the fruit thereof, and did eat, and gave also unto her husband with her; and he did eat. And the eyes of both of them were opened" (Genesis 3:6-7).

Satan is after souls. Satan is among the saints, ever trying.

Why did Satan approach Eve first? Adam was the *head* of the home. Eve was the *heart* of the home. Satan was wise enough to realize that if he could get the heart, he would take the citadel, the fortress, the stronghold, and capture the whole family. Ladies, beware! Beware of Satan among the saints.

Satan is among the saints *to steal away the Word from the hearers, lest they believe!* The parable of the sower in Luke 8:5-15 reveals this fact. Let us apply it to the minister and congregation.

91

The sanctuary was crowded. In fact it was filled to overflowing. The members were present. It looked as though each family of the membership was accompanied by visitors. The canvassing of various neighborhoods with invitations to visit the church had definitely brought results. The minister was inspired and elated as he took his place in the pulpit to preach the Word.

Some of the Word fell on wayside hearts. These were people who heard but who allowed the devil to take away the Word out of their hearts, lest they should believe and be saved. Mark 4:12 describes them like this: "That seeing they may see, and not perceive; and hearing they may hear, and not understand; lest at any time they should be converted, and their sins should be forgiven them."

Some of the preached Word fell upon rocky, hard hearts in the congregation. It tried to take hold, but the new plant withered, because it lacked attention. These people heard the Word and received it, but they did not allow it to take root. James 1:19 exhorts, "Let every man be swift to hear."

Some of the Word fell among thorns, and the thorns sprang up with it and choked it. These people heard the Word and went forth, but the new plant was choked with cares, riches, and pleasures of this life, and they did not bring fruit to perfection. "Bring forth therefore fruits worthy of repentance. . . . Now also the axe is laid unto the root of the trees: every tree therefore which bringeth not forth good fruit is hewn down, and cast into the fire" (Luke 3:8-9).

The minister continued sowing the Word. "And other fell on good ground [the receptive hearts], and sprang up, and bare fruit an hundredfold. . . . But that on the good ground are they, which in an honest and good heart, having heard the word, keep it, and bring forth fruit with patience" (Luke 8:8, 15).

Jesus said, "The words that I speak unto you, they are spirit, and they are life" (John 6:63). Peter told Jesus, "Lord, . . . thou hast the words of eternal life" (John 6:68).

When Jesus finished the parable of the sower, He cried, "He that hath ears to hear, let him hear. . . . Take heed therefore how ye hear: for whosoever hath, to him shall be given; and whosoever hath not, from him shall be taken even that which he seemeth to have" (Luke 8:8, 18.)

Satan is *among* the saints, not *in* the saints. He visited the assembly in Job's day. He influenced and connived with Ananias and Sapphira in their home. He went with them to the First Church of Jerusalem, where he put it in their hearts to lie to the Holy Ghost. He brought about the circumstances that caused their death. He went into the Garden of Eden and worked on Eve's mind, bringing about the downfall of her and Adam.

We must face the fact that the enemy does visit our congregations. He already has the people of the world in which he roams. The church is a fertile field for the souls he wants to overcome. Each of us should be alert to his tactics in order not to lend ourselves to his workings. He has no good cause in mind when he finds himself among the saints.

He also knows when he is in the company of people who are unsaved. People from all walks of life attend our services, searching for something to satisfy their longing, something solid to lean upon.

93

Are you receptive to their needs? Are you reverent, worshipful, and prayerfully attentive to the leading of the Spirit so that He may do a work in the hearts of people? Do not withhold yourself, your testimony, your prayer, your consecration, and the giving of your offerings and tithes.

It is heartbreaking to see some who whisper in church, drop a song book, rearrange their hair, chew gum, go through their purse, and even get up and walk out. Satan can use these tactics to distract people's mind from the preaching of the Word. Do not be guilty of playing into his hands, of allowing him to have a grand time as he steals the Word from the hearers, lest they believe. They may never come back.

The service from which you withhold participation could be the most important one for some people. They may have come because of an invitation. Perhaps some are there for the beautiful singing. They may be affected when they hear and see the singers with tears coursing down their cheeks. We ought to give careful attention, give all we are, all we have, and our very best every time we assemble.

Nothing is sacred to the enemy. He rushes in where angels fear to tread. Let us consider one more example: Jesus and His twelve apostles. This was one of the most sacred groups ever to assemble. If there was ever to be a hedge around anyone, it seems it should have been around these thirteen men. The twelve apostles had left all to follow Jesus. In Mark 8:29 we read Peter's confession of faith: "Thou art the Christ." Then Jesus began to teach them that He must suffer many things, be rejected by the elders, chief priests, and scribes, and be killed, whereupon Peter began to rebuke him. Jesus rebuked Peter, saying, "Get thee behind me, Satan: for thou savourest not the things that be of God, but the things that be of men" (Mark 8:33). Satan was among the saints. Peter loved the Lord and had just confessed faith in Him. Never did he think he could be used of Satan to discourage and weaken Jesus in the cause for which He was ordained, but immediately after his confession he allowed Satan to influence his thoughts and words.

John 13 tells us about the last Passover feast kept by Jesus and the Twelve, His washing of the disciples' feet, and His prediction of His betrayal. These events show us how close Jesus felt to His disciples. He wanted them to share with him. John 13:2 reads, "And supper being ended, the devil [Satan among the saints] having now put into the heart of Judas Iscariot to betray him . . ." Verse 30 makes a short statement after the departure of Judas: "And it was night." Yet with all the shadows within that statement, Jesus' heart had grown light, for His next words were, "Now is the Son of man glorified" (John 13:31).

These examples show the lengths Satan will resort to in order to gain a soul. We must never underestimate the Wicked One. God can put a hedge around any one of us if and when necessary. He is attentive to His children. That does not mean we will always escape the tests of life, but we can count on God to look on us lovingly and to care for us. He does not allow more on us than we can bear, but will with every temptation make a way of escape (I Corinthians 10:13).

Jesus knows that Satan is at work among the saints, and we have the promise of Jude 24-25: "Now unto him that is able to keep you from falling, and to present you faultless before the presence of his glory with exceeding joy, to the only wise God our Saviour."

There are some things only the Master can do!

5

THOU HAST MAGNIFIED THY WORD ABOVE THY NAME

Psalm 138:1-2

Outline

I. The People of the Name
   A. Love for the name
   B. Love for the Word
   C. Salvation in the name

II. God Looks at Names
   A. He changed Abram's name
   B. He changed Jacob's name
   C. He changed Saul's name
   D. He changed Sarai's name
   E. The name of Jesus

III. The Word Is Exalted above the Name
   From the pen of David

IV. God Honored the Word
   A. Fulfillment of Scripture (Micah 5:2)
   B. Prophecy in the Word of Jesus' birth (Matthew 2:13-15)
   C. "Out of Egypt have I called my son" (see Hosea 11:1)

V. Men Who Ignored Portions of the Word
   A. Achan
   B. Saul

VI. Keeping the Word
   A. Jesus' promise at the Ascension
   B. Moses and Zipporah Kept the Word

C. Jesus honored the Word when tempted by Satan

VII. We Must Keep the Word
A. Teachings of Jesus
B. I Corinthians 6:6-8
C. Mark 13:38; 14:38

VIII. David Honored the Word
A. David and Saul
B. Not just for David
C. Mordecai, King Ahasuerus, and Haman

IX. The Word and the Law of Forgiveness
The Word is forever settled in heaven

X. Psalm 138:1-2

THOU HAST MAGNIFIED THY WORD ABOVE THY NAME

I will praise thee with my whole heart: before the gods will I sing praise unto thee. I will worship toward thy holy temple, and praise thy name for thy lovingkindness and for thy truth: for thou hast magnified thy word above all thy name (Psalm 138:1-2).

God's people love His name. They love His Word, and there is no shortage of Bibles among them, yet it is easy to overlook certain truths in many passages of Scriptures. Maybe we overlook a part of Scripture because one great truth will stand out to us and overshadow the rest of the verse.

The ministers preach and teach the fundamentals. They contend for the faith once delivered to the saints (Jude 3), but there are some things in the Word that God would have us to refresh our thinking about. He would like to impress us with this thought: His Word is magnified above His name!

Not one of us would ever take anything away from that glorious, wonderful, majestic, saving name of Jesus Christ. We love that name above all names. "Neither is there salvation in any other: for there is none other name under heaven given among men, whereby we must be saved" (Acts 4:12). It is no wonder, and it is with reason, that we believe in and love that name.

God thinks and looks at names in ways that are different from our thoughts. God changed Abram's name to Abraham, which means "father of a great multitude." "Neither shall thy name any more be called Abram, but thy name shall be Abraham; for a father of many nations have I made thee" (Genesis 17:5). It would not have made a difference with most people if he had been called Abram forever.

God changed Jacob's name, which means "supplanter," to Israel, meaning "a prince of God," "for as a prince hast thou power with God and with men, and hast prevailed" (Genesis 32:28). We know that "supplanter" fits Jacob because of the way he obtained the birthright from Esau. Supplanter also had a good meaning: Jacob, or Israel, followed in Abraham and Isaac's foosteps and became a planter of nations. Would it have made any difference with people if he had always been known as Jacob? It made a difference with God!

Why was Saul's name changed to Paul? We know Saul as a persecutor. The name Paul or Paulus means "little." In Paul's own sight he considered himself the least. "Unto me, who am less than the least of all saints, is this grace given, that I should preach among the Gentiles the unsearchable riches of Christ" (Ephesians 3:8). We know Paul as the apostle to the Gentiles.

These changes of names followed a great change in a person's life and signified a special work by a person yielded to God's will. God let them know that He was mindful of them.

He also changed Sarai's name to Sarah, which means "princess." "And God said unto Abraham, As for Sarai thy wife, thou shalt not call her name Sarai, but Sarah shall her name be. And I will bless her and give thee a son also of her: yea, I will bless her, and she shall be a mother of nations; kings of people shall be of her" (Genesis 17:15-16). Sarah was just as much a part of the promise as Abraham was. (See Genesis 17:17-22.)

The name of Jesus means "Jehovah-Savior." "And she shall bring forth a son, and thou shalt call his name JESUS: for he shall save his people from their sin" (Matthew 1:21).

We love God's name! We must never minimize the importance, the greatness, the power, and the essentiality of the name of Jesus. That name has separated us from all other churches. We contend for the name of Jesus. It is the name that makes us different from any other people in all the world. There are people who preach receiving the Holy Ghost, speaking in tongues, but who do not preach the name! As ministers and people, we should be willing to give our lives before denying the name of Jesus.

"Thou hast magnified thy word above all thy name" came from the pen of David, sweet singer in Israel, a man after God's own heart, and into the Bible. Holy men of old wrote as they were moved by the Holy Ghost (II Peter 1:21). David knew that the Spirit of God was moving him to exalt the Word of God. He wanted everyone who read this verse, or heard it quoted, to know how important the Word really is and how highly exalted it is. He wanted to lift it as high as possible. Had he said the Word was exalted above the tallest mountain peak, that would be high to us. If he had written that God's Word is exalted above the moon, we would get some idea of how high his Word is exalted. Had he written that it was above the sun, the stars, the sky, we would have accepted it as being gloriously magnified. It seems he wanted to lift the Word even higher, and yet higher still. What better way to lift the Word than to exalt and magnify it above the name of the Savior of the world?

Let us notice how the biblical writers, under the inspiration of the Holy Ghost, introduced subjects they wanted to place strong emphasis upon. For example, Paul seemed to exert every ounce of knowledge and writing ability that he possessed to magnify, glorify, and stress the importance of charity, or love. He used subjects known to the people to get his point across.

We believe in speaking with tongues. Many cherish the gift of tongues. Yet Paul said if we speak with the tongues of men and of angels and have not love, it is become as sounding brass or a twinkling cymbal. Throughout I Corinthians 13 he tried to show the importance of love.

Eventually he concluded, "Now abideth faith, hope, charity, these three; but the greatest of these is charity" (I Corinthians 13:13). Paul was not minimizing the essentiality of faith and hope; rather he was using two of the strongest essentials to place strong emphasis on the subject of love.

We know that without faith it is impossible to please God (Hebrew 11:6). We are saved by faith and hope. Paul used these two strong elements to build his platform to the top step: now abide faith, hope, and love, but the *greatest* of these is love. Paul knew that we would accept the first two strong essentials, and by accepting them in the way he presented them, we would not overlook the importance of charity, or love.

The author of Hebrews introduced the glorious plan of salvation in a similar manner: "If the word spoken by angels was stedfast"—and everyone, even sinners, will acknowledge that. "For if the word spoken by angels was stedfast, and every transgression and disobedience received a just recompense of reward; how shall we escape, if we neglect so great salvation?" (Hebrews 2:2-3).

David, under the inspiration of the Holy Ghost, used the same method and wisdom to stress the importance of the Word. David knew that God's people love His name. But he let us know that God's Word is magnified above His name. This statement does not detract from the name of Jesus, because "the Word was made flesh, and dwelt among us" (John 1:14), and the name of the manifested Word was Jesus!

Were it not for the Word of God, we would know nothing about the name of Jesus. It would be no more than any other name. Because the Word exalts the name, it moves us to love the name. The Word says, "Thou shalt call his name JESUS: for he shall save his people from their sins" (Matthew 1:21). The Word says, "There is none other name under heaven given among men, whereby we must be saved" (Acts 4:12).

We love the Word. We adhere to the Word, yet there are portions of it that we sometimes overlook, parts that are necessary. We cannot take just a part; we must accept all of the Word of God.

God has honored verses that to us may actually seem of little or no significance. For example, in Micah 5:2, God inserted a verse for us to read that meant nothing to the world. It was of little importance to anyone, but that verse said the Son of God would be born in Bethlehem. "But thou, Bethlehem Ephratah, though thou be little among the thousands of Judah, yet out of thee shall he come forth unto me that is to be ruler in Israel; whose goings forth have been from of old, from everlasting." We would love Him if He had been born anywhere, but God respected that verse and fulfilled it. It may have been overlooked by others, but not by God. It was in His word, and He does not overlook one portion of the Word. He will honor and keep His Word.

When it came time for Jesus to be born, Joseph and Mary were living in Galilee, but they had to go to Bethlehem for Jesus' birth. It was absolutely essential and necessary that Jesus be born in Bethlehem. No matter the discomfort of Mary as she was heavy with child; no matter the sacrifice of Joseph in getting her there. The most important thing was that she be in Bethlehem for the birth of Jesus. God honored the fulfillment of His Word.

Similarly, the Bible tells us how to be born again if we want to enter the kingdom of God. You may overlook it. It may seem of no significance to you. You may turn to John 3:16 and stop there, but God's Word says, "Except a man be born again, he cannot see the kingdom of God" (John 3:3).

The Lord upholds verses that we may feel are of no importance, or unnecessary. He is mindful of every word, to the dotting of the i and the crossing of the t.

While Jesus was yet a babe, God fulfilled another verse that perhaps no one else would take note of. In Matthew 2:13-15 we read:

And when they [the wise men from the East] were departed, behold, the angel of the Lord appeareth to Joseph in a dream, saying, Arise, and take the young child and his mother, and flee into Egypt, and be thou there until I bring thee word: for Herod will seek the young child to destroy him. When he arose, he took the young child and his mother by night, and departed into Egypt: and was there until the death of Herod: that it might be fulfilled which was spoken of the Lord by the prophet, saying, Out of Egypt have I called my son.

The words quoted are from Hosea 11:1. This passage illustrates the truth that prophetic utterances often have a deeper meaning than at first appears. God honored His Word. Let us be careful not to dishonor it, for if God keeps His Word, how much more should we! The Lord saw to it that they went down into Egypt and stayed there until He called them out, in fulfillment of that verse. Would that have been of importance to any of us? We would have probably gone to sleep on hearing the prophet preach on that subject before the birth of Christ!

Some people of the Old Testament ignored portions of the Word of God, and it cost them very much.

Consider Achan. He had to be under the age of twenty—just a little boy—when the Israelites drew back from entering Canaan and began forty years of wandering in the wilderness. Only two men over the age of twenty at that time eventually reached Canaan: Joshua and Caleb.

By the time Achan entered the pages of God's Word, he was married and had children. The Israelites had not been in Canaan very long. Achan certainly remembered their miraculous crossing of the Jordan River as well as miracles God did in the wilderness. He remembered the pillar of cloud by day for shade, and the pillar of fire by night to give them light and to keep the enemy at a distance.

Undoubtedly, he told his children about the miracles

he had seen. He could remind them about crossing Jordan on dry land behind the ark of the covenant of God carried by the priests. When he returned from Jericho, did he tell them about marching around the walls for six days, and on the seventh day walking around seven times and shouting until the walls fell flat? His testimony would have held any audience spellbound! He believed in God.

He could tell what Jehovah had done for them. He had a story to tell, a ministry to shout about. This man, Achan, with all his experiences that he could reminisce over and share with others, overlooked one single statement: When God gives you the city of Jericho, leave the accursed thing alone, and put the gold and silver into the treasury of the Lord. (See Joshua 6:18-19.)

This Israelite, who so enjoyed the blessings of God, overlooked one statement of God. It seemed of no importance to him. But God meant what He said. Achan's disobedience cost his life and the lives of all related to him. They were stoned to death and their bodies burned with fire (Joshua 7:25). It cost Achan to ignore part of God's Word. All the blessings he had enjoyed, all that he believed about Jehovah, his testimony and ministry, and then the shame and disgrace he brought upon his kindred—he took these memories into an endless eternity because he overlooked one statement of God. Achan's life is written into the Word as an example to us. Let us give heed to the Word!

King Saul is another who overlooked a part of the Word. Saul was chosen of God from among many men. Countless men would have treasured the honor of being crowned king of Israel. Saul was the one selected, because he stood high in the sight of God. It is true that he stood head and shoulders above others, but that is not why he was tall in God's sight. At this time he was a small or little man in his own sight. Therefore, God selected him to be the king of Israel.

Immediately after being chosen, he must have acquainted himself with some valuable and treasured portions of Scripture. He found that a wizard should be put to death (Leviticus 20:27). He also found that people were to worship God and not idols (Leviticus 19:4). He had all the idols destroyed. He was mindful of the Word of God. He not only wanted to obey but he did obey. He carried out the Word to the crossing of the t and the dotting of the i.

Saul was a giant in the sight of men and of God. Now the Lord was going to use him to keep a promise that God made to Moses some four hundred years ago. God had Samuel to tell Saul to mobilize the army and destroy all the Amalekites, all of their oxen, and all of their possessions. Saul gathered an army of 210,000 men. He called them together and spoke to all the people. He told the Kenites, "You are living among us, dwelling in our land. You were kind to the Israelites. We want you to separate yourselves from the Amalekites. We are giving you the opportunity to come out from among them, for they are doomed!" Saul gave the Kenites plenty of time, and they did separate themselves.

When Saul and his army began slaying the Amalekites—men, women, boys, girls, animals—he slew them from Havilah to Shur. Finally, the day was over. God spoke to Samuel that night, and said, "I repent that I ever anointed Saul King of Israel." Samuel wept all night, arose, and went to meet Saul.

Saul said to Samuel, "Blessed be thou of the LORD: I have performed the commandment of the LORD" (I Samuel 15:13). Some sheep began to bleat, some cattle began to low, and Samuel asked, "What then is the meaning of this bleating of sheep and lowing of cattle?" Saul answered, "Oh, the people have kept back the best to sacrifice to the Lord, and the rest we have utterly destroyed."

Saul thought that excuse would be valid and acceptable to God. He was king of Israel. If he wanted to keep back some of the best, he thought, it would be appropriate for the king to do so.

Saul, who had all the wizards destroyed, who removed and destroyed all the idols from the land to comply with the Word of the Lord, overlooked one little word. God said destroy *all!* He did not say nearly all, or ninety-five percent. Saul, the Word of God is magnified above His name.

In passing, let us make an application of the part of the story about the Kenites, whom Saul allowed to separate themselves from the Amalekites before their destruction. No doubt there are many friends among us. Perhaps you are one. You cherish our friendship as we treasure yours. You are not one of us, but you are among us. If you go to church, you go to one of our faith. You give to our church, missions, and work of God. We ask you to come out from among the world. Separate yourself, and cast your lot with the people of God. The world is doomed. God's Word is true!

Before ascending to heaven, in Luke 24:49 Jesus said, "Behold I send the promise of my Father upon you: but tarry ye in the city of Jerusalem, until ye be endued with power from on high." This promise was fulfilled in Acts 2:4: "And they were all filled with the Holy Ghost, and began to speak with other tongues, as the Spirit gave them utterance." Now let us read Acts 2:37-39.

Now when they [the people in the audience] heard this, they were pricked in their heart, and said unto Peter and to the rest of the apostles, Men and brethren, what shall we do? Then Peter said unto them, Repent, and be baptized every one of you in the name of Jesus Christ for the remission of sins, and ye shall receive the gift of the Holy Ghost. For the promise is unto you, and to your children, and to all that are afar off, even as many as the Lord our God shall call.

Has he called you? The promise is for all. It is His Word. And His Word is magnified above His name.

Moses identified himself with Israel at an early age. "And it came to pass in those days, when Moses was grown, that he went out unto his brethren, and looked on their burdens: and he spied an Egyptian smiting an Hebrew, one of his brethren. And he looked this way and that way, and when he saw that there was no man, he slew the Egyptian, and hid him in the sand" (Exodus 2:11-12). Now God did not want Moses slaying, but saving, people. Moses had to flee to Midian and dwell there until God commissioned him to lead the Israelites out of Egyptian bondage.

Every excuse Moses offered, God offset it. Moses was fearful; God said, "I will be with you." Moses said, "I can't speak"; God said, "I will give you a spokesman. Take Aaron with you." (See Exodus 4.) Moses finally started to Egypt to lead God's people out.

According to God's covenant with Abraham and his descendants, every male child was to be circumcised; those who were not were to be separated from among the Israelites (Genesis 17:9-14). Moses failed to respect that law.

And it came to pass by the way in the inn, that the LORD met him, and sought to kill him. Then Zipporah took a sharp stone, and cut off the foreskin of her son, and cast it at his feet, and said, Surely a bloody husband art thou to me. So he let him go: then she said, A bloody husband thou art, because of the circumcision (Exodus 4:24-26).

Did Zipporah resent circumcision? How did she know about it? As a Midianite, Zipporah was a descendant of Abraham and his wife Keturah (Genesis 25:1-2). She did not forget, and Moses surely should not have overlooked, this law. Could it be that Zipporah lost some respect for Moses regarding this?

Jesus respected and honored the Word. Never once did He change, alter or fail to fulfill the Word.

Immediately after being baptized, Jesus was led into the wilderness, where He fasted for forty days and nights. (See Luke 4:1-13.) He afterward hungered. He must have been very weak in body. The devil said to Him, "Command this stone that it be made bread." Jesus answered, "It is written, That man shall not live by bread alone, but by every word of God."

The devil took Him up to a high mountain, showed Him all the kingdoms of the world in a moment of time, and said to Him, "If thou therefore wilt worship me, all shall be thine." Jesus answered, "It is written, Thou shalt worship the Lord thy God and him only shalt thou serve."

Satan then brought him to a pinnacle of the Temple in Jerusalem, saying, "Cast thyself down from hence: for it is written, He shall give his angels charge over thee, to keep thee." Yes, Satan quoted Jesus' words, "It is written." This time Jesus answered, "It is said, Thou shalt not tempt the Lord thy God."

The devil then departed from Him—for a season.

Jesus honored the words penned by David, "Thou hast magnified thy word above all thy name."

The purpose of this message is to try to get you to think about any little verse or part of a verse that you are not respecting, that you are failing to keep. See it as God looks at it. He will not overlook that you failed to keep it. It is His Word, and He has magnified His Word above His name.

Let us consider some teachings of Jesus. "I say unto you which hear, Love your enemies, do good to them which hate you, bless them that curse you, and pray for them which despitefully use you" (Luke 6:27-28). "As ye would that men should do to you, do ye also to them likewise" (Luke 6:31). We should shout about the name of Jesus, but at the same time remember that Jesus said, "Love your enemies, do good to them that hate you."

Are you having trouble loving somebody? There is a remedy in the Bible. You will have no more trouble loving that person if you will pray for him every day, sincerely pray for him. Call his name in prayer.

We have come through the Acts of the Apostles. We have experienced Acts 2:38: repentance, baptism in His name, and the infilling of the Holy Ghost. We are evangelizing the world just as the people in the Book of Acts did! We are the people of the name! But let us read I Corinthians 6:6-8: "Brother goeth to law with brother, and that before unbelievers. Now therefore there is utterly a fault among you, because ye go to law one with another. Why do ye not rather take wrong? why do ye not rather suffer yourselves to be defrauded? Nay, ye do wrong, and defraud, and that your brethren."

Is it hard to smile when you read or hear that preached? Would you rather frown and close your ears? Preachers did not say it. God said it! If we want to make it to heaven, we had better obey! His Word is magnified above His name. It is wonderful, it is good to wear His name if we keep His Word.

Jesus said, "Watch and pray" (Mark 13:33; 14:38). Prayer is the key to obeying God's Word. When we pray we can watch the Lord take care of our situation. When we pray He will remove any dross or impurity from our heart, mind, and soul. In reality that is what prayer is all about. Prayer does not change God. Prayer changes us! That is why Jesus went to Gethsemane. It was not to have the cross removed. He knew the cross was His when He was born. It was ever before Him. He went to Gethsemane to pray to be able to submit to the cross. In prayer He sobbed, "Not my will, but thine, be done" (Luke 22:42).

Many people have problems with some of the things we have mentioned. We all have our friends, and we do not need our enemies. But we need to love them. As we would that people would do to us, we are to do to them. God honors that kind of attitude. He puts us on our honor.

There is not a one of us who does not know how we would like to be treated. God gave a very simple, understandable instruction on how to treat our enemy or anyone else: Do unto others as you would have them do unto you.

If you had the awesome, tremendous, and sometimes even gruesome responsibility of superintending the United Pentecostal Church International do you have any idea how you would like for people to treat you? God is placing us on our honor. Do not think He does not judge us in this area.

Let us look at a biblical example. Saul was backslidden, and God had already anointed David to be king. Saul was seeking the life of David. David knew it. He knew beyond any possible shadow of doubt that if Saul could lay his hands on him, it would be the end for him. Saul came off his throne and sought the life of David. One night during the hunt Saul fell asleep, and God saw to it that he slept soundly.

God was putting one of His servants to a test. This servant had passed a lot of tests. The Lord let a lion attack him and he killed it. The Lord let a bear charge him and he killed it. The Lord allowed him to slay a giant. It is easy to kill a lion or a bear, compared to killing the carnal man. David now faced the supreme test required to graduate in God's school.

The Lord put him to a real test. Saul was asleep on the ground. David and his men came up to where Saul was sleeping. David knew what Saul would do to him if he had the chance. But one statement from God—and that is all we need—stopped David from taking Saul's life: "Touch not mine anointed, and do my prophets no harm" (Psalm 105:15). Saul had been the anointed of God.

115

David decided to honor the Word of God. The servant saw that he was reluctant to do what he wanted to do, so the servant said, "Just say the word and I will pin him to the ground." Many times we will back off from doing something, but we are glad to see someone else do it. But David said no. Some would crown David for killing the bear, the lion, and the giant, but here is where we should crown him. David went from that experience to the throne of Israel as king.

That verse was not only given to David. It is not just for the laity. If any of us, including ministers, shout about the name, and then murder, ridicule, backbite, and talk about our brother and sister in the Lord then we do not honor God's Word. But God has magnified the Word above His name.

This verse does not only refer to preachers. There are also the saints of God, whom He has anointed with the Holy Ghost. We should be afraid to ridicule them. We should love them and feed them. When they are in trouble, we do not want to put our foot on them and push them down. We want to pick them up and help them along the way. They are anointed of God with the Holy Ghost. The verse says touch not God's anointed and do His prophets no harm.

Let us examine someone who failed to respect that verse. Mordecai was a Jew in a Gentile kingdom ruled by King Ahasuerus. Haman was a very jealous man who had the ear of the king and who hated Mordecai. He saw to it that a law was passed to put all Jews to death. Someone suggested that he build a gallows and have Mordecai hanged. He had the gallows built; all he needed was the king's permission to kill Mordecai. He sought a session to ask for the king's permission. But then God took over.

One night the king asked for the royal scroll to be read to him. It recorded that on a certain day a plot was made against the king. Mordecai discovered it, told Esther (his cousin and the queen), and Esther told the king. The plotters were put to death and the king's life was spared. When that account was read King Ahasuerus asked, "Was that man ever rewarded for his deed?" The answer was that nothing had been done. At that time there was a noise outside the door. "Who is that outside?" the king asked. The servants said, "My lord, it is Haman." The king asked for him to come in.

Haman thought he was so important that he did not even have to ask for an audience. He thought he was going to get what he wanted. But no, he was going to get what he wanted the other man to get. We had better be careful of the thoughts we allow ourselves to think about others.

The king said, "Haman, there is a man I want to honor. I want you to tell me how to honor this man." Selfish Haman thought, Who would the king want to honor beside me? Me! That is our greatest enemy. Haman, thinking it was himself the king wished to honor, said, "Clothe him in the king's garments, put him on the horse that the king rides, set the royal crown on his head, parade him through the streets of the city, and proclaim before him, 'Thus shall it be done to him whom the king delights to honor.'" That is what Haman wanted for himself!

Now let us watch how God reversed this. Proverbs 28:10 says that a wicked man will fall into his own pit. The king said, "All right. You do this to Mordecai and don't miss one thing that you said." How Haman wished he had suggested something else!

Ultimately, it was Haman who ended up hanging on the gallows. Haman built the gallows for Mordecai and wanted to ride the streets of the city on the king's horse, but Mordecai got the horse and Haman got the gallows! If we do not respect God's Word He can reverse it against us.

Someone's name would have no value were it not for his word. The person makes the name what it is. Likewise, the Word of God has made the name of God what it is.

God's Word says, "Be ye therefore merciful, as your Father also is merciful. Judge not, and ye shall not be judged. Condemn not, and ye shall not be condemned: forgive, and ye shall be forgiven" (Luke 6:36-37). Do we honor these words?

Peter once asked Jesus how strictly we needed to follow this teaching. "Lord, how oft shall my brother sin against me, and I forgive him? till seven times? Jesus saith unto him, I say not unto thee, Until seven times: but, Until seventy times seven" (Matthew 18:21-22). So many want to multiply those numbers and stop there. But the meaning of this statement is that there is no end to forgiveness.

Jesus followed this statement with a very beautiful parable:

Therefore is the kingdom of heaven likened unto a certain king, which took account of his servants. And, when he had begun to reckon, one was brought unto him, which owed him ten thousand talents [millions of dollars]. But forasmuch as he had not to pay, his lord commanded him to be sold, and his wife, and children, and all that he had, and payment to be made. The servant therefore fell down, and worshipped him, saying, Lord, have patience with me, and I will pay thee all. Then the lord of that servant was moved with compassion, and loosed him, and forgave him the debt. But the same servant went out, and found one of his fellowservants, which owed him an hundred pence [a few dollars]: and he laid hands on him, and took him by the throat, saying, Pay me that thou owest. And his fellowservant fell down at his feet, and besought him, saying, Have patience with me, and I will pay thee all. And he would not: but went and cast him into prison, till he should pay the debt. So when his fellowservants saw what was done, they were very sorry, and came and told unto their lord all that was done. Then his lord, after that he had called him, said unto him, O thou wicked servant, I forgave thee all that debt, because thou desiredst me: Shouldest not thou also have had compassion on thy fellowservant, even as I had pity on thee? And his lord was wroth, and delivered him to the tormentors, till he should pay all that was due unto him. So likewise shall my heavenly Father do also unto you, if ye from your hearts forgive not every one his brother their trespasses (Matthew 18:28-35).

This example ought to move all of us to be forgiving. The Lord forgave us so much. We will never have to forgive anyone more than God forgave us.

The Word of God is forever settled in heaven! (Psalm 119:89).

"I will praise thee with my whole heart: before the gods will I sing praise unto thee. I will worship toward thy holy temple, and praise thy name for thy lovingkindness and for thy truth: for thou hast magnified thy word above all thy name."

119

6

THE ACCURACY OF GOD'S WORD

II Peter 3:4-7

Outline

Introduction: By the Word of God the heavens and earth were of old. By the same Word they are kept in store. His Word is just as powerful today.

I. The Accuracy of God's Word in the Scientific World
   A. In the beginning God created, God spoke
   B. Facts about the earth
      1. The earth is one of the nine major planets
      2. Fifth in size, 25,000 miles in circumference, 8,000 miles in diameter
      3. It moves around the sun at the speed of 66,000 miles per hour
      4. It rotates every 23 hours, 36 minutes, 4.1 seconds; its regularity
      5. Satellites and space ships are launched based on the accuracy of the earth's rotation

II. The Natural and Physical Kingdom
   A. The natural world operates by God's Word
      1. Colt tied to a hitching post (Luke 19:30)
      2. Last Supper: man with pitcher of water (Mark 14:13)
      3. Taxes: fish with gold in its mouth (Matthew 17:27)
   B. Healing
      1. Centurion's servant: "Speak the word only" (Matthew 8:8)
      2. The nobleman's son: healed "at the same hour" (John 4:53)

III. The Spiritual Kingdom
   A. Jesus did not die to set up a scientific kingdom
      God created the heavens and earth before Calvary
   B. Jesus did not die to set up a physical kingdom
      People were healed before Calvary
   C. The Lord did die to set up a spiritual kingdom
      1. The promise as He ascended (Luke 24:49)
      2. The promise fulfilled: Day of Pentecost (Acts 2)
         a. Jewish nation (Acts 2:1-41)
         b. Gentile people (Acts 10)

IV. Christ Jesus Died For You!
   A. The Word—a sure foundation!
   B. The accuracy of God's Word

The Accuracy of God's Word

*And saying, Where is the promise of his coming? for
since the fathers fell asleep, all things continue as they were
from the beginning of creation. For this they willingly are
ignorant of, that by the word of God the heavens were of
old, and the earth standing out of the water and in the
water: whereby the world that then was, being overflowed
with water, perished: but the heavens and the earth, which
are now, by the same world are kept in store, reserved unto
fire against the day of judgment and perdition of ungodly
man* (II Peter 3:4-7).

Verse 5 reminds us that God by His powerful Word
created the heavens and earth and put everything in its
place. He divided the earth from the firmament and divided the light from the darkness—all by His Word! He took
nothing and made the world, and He hung it on nothing.
He put the world on its course and told it to stay there.

Verse 7 tells us that the heavens and earth are kept
by that same powerful Word. Thousands of years ago God
spoke them into existence. His same powerful Word is
still holding them in place.

This earth on which we live is one of the nine large
planets in our solar system. It is fifth in size. In round
figures the earth is some 25,000 miles in circumference.
We have lived to see men go to the moon and take pictures of the earth from the moon. Our earth is round
(almost). There is just as much space under it as there
is above it. In diameter, the earth is about 8,000 miles.

That is the size of the planet earth on which we live.
It is small compared to the space there is—unlimited

space. The Lord created it, flung it out into space, set it on its course, and said, "Stay there." All that is holding this earth in place is the Word of God. There is nothing underneath it. Everything on earth has something to hold it up. The foundation of a building holds the building up, but there is nothing holding up the earth.

We refer to Australia as being "underneath" because of its location on the globe. In Australia, underneath the earth, people stand just as we stand in North America. They look up to see the sky, the sun, the moon, the stars, just as people in North America, but it is considered as being underneath. What a miraculous God we serve!

Some people believe that the sun goes around the earth. That is not true. The earth goes around the sun, traveling around the sun at the staggering, amazing, almost unbelievable speed of 66,000 miles an hour! That is how fast we are traveling right now on this planet around the sun—traveling so fast yet it does not disturb us whatsoever! It does not disturb the waters of the sea, the rivers, the lakes, or the streams.

We can draw water from a well, pour it into a bucket, take the bucket by the handle, carry it wherever we want to place it, and never lose a drop. The earth's turning does not disturb anything that is on the earth.

While the earth is traveling around the sun, it rotates. Every twenty-three hours, fifty-six minutes, four and one-tenth seconds, it rotates. We get our day from the rotation of the earth, which is held to the tenth of a second. It never digresses, it never varies. Nothing is holding it. Nothing is controlling it but the Word of God. Are we afraid to stand on it? No, never, we just take it all for granted.

Some years ago a satellite was placed 22,300 miles above Brazil. It moved in the form of the numeral eight. This path put it within reach of ninety percent of the free world all the time for the transmission of pictures and messages.

For early space travel the correct orbital path was selected for launching into space. The launch was planned with the return trip in mind. The spaceship went into space on a certain trajectory in order to return on the correct path.

Scientists could plan this because of the accuracy of the rotation of the earth. And nothing controls it but the Word of God! Some know-it-all may look you in the face and say, "I don't believe it." Nevertheless, it is true. I am so glad to be standing on the Word, believing in it, trusting in it!

We have noted the accuracy of God's Word in the scientific realm. Let us also look at biblical examples of the accuracy of God's Word in the natural kingdom. God's Word is accurate in natural things that do not pertain to the salvation of the soul or the healing of the body.

Jesus once said to His disciples, "Go over into the village and you will find a colt tied at a hitching post. I want you to untie the colt and bring it to me." The disciples reacted just as we probably would have: "Whose colt is it? What is the owner going to say?" Jesus, knowing their thinking, said, "While you are untying that colt the owner will say to you, 'Why are you untying my colt?' Just tell him that I have need of it and then bring it to Me."

How would you like to go on a mission like that? If you do not enjoy knocking on doors to invite people to church, you would not like being sent on a mission like that. The disciples went to the village and looked, and there was the hitching post. The colt was tied to it just exactly as His Word said! They could have looked at one another and said, "So far, so good." We can depend on God's Word and say, "So far, so good." It has never failed!

They walked up to the colt and began untying it. While they were unfastening it, the owner asked, "Why are you untying my colt?" just as Jesus had said. They answered him as Jesus told them to. We should not be afraid to say what Jesus tells us to say. They said, "The Lord needs it," untied the colt, and took it to the Master.

The Lord knew who to allow to own a colt so that He could get it when He wanted it. That could be the reason some of us do not have more: the Lord knows He could not get it when He wants it. That may be why some people have certain things: He may want it there where He knows He can get it if He asks for it. He knows who to give to, and who to withhold from. This example relates to the natural kingdom, not to salvation at all.

On another occasion Jesus said to Peter and John, "It is time for us to keep the Passover. Go prepare a place for the Passover." They were not in Capernaum where Peter lived. They were not where John lived. They looked at each other and asked, "Where can we prepare a place for the Passover?" He said, "Go and you will meet a man carrying a pitcher of water."

In those days, a man did not normally carry a pitcher of water; women did that job. It was the young lady Rebekah who went to draw the water. It was the Samaritan woman at the well who was drawing water. All through the Old and New Testament, it was the women who went to the well to draw water. People could see women coming from the common well on the streets with pitchers of water on their shoulders, but they did not see men carrying water.

Nevertheless, Jesus told Peter and John that they would see a man carrying a pitcher of water. He told them to follow that man to the house he entered, and say to the owner of the house, "The Master says to you, 'Where is the guest room where I shall eat the Passover with My disciples?'"

This event pertains to natural things. God controls natural things. He is interested in natural things that pertain to our lives. He is not just interested in our souls, but He is also interested in our natural welfare. If we give Him what belongs to Him, He will take care of us.

Peter and John went into the village. There came the man with the pitcher of water. So far, so good. None of His words have ever failed yet, nor will they ever fail.

Peter and John turned around to follow the man. When he saw two men turning around and following him, he may have thought, I'll be glad to get to my street. When he did get to the place and turned off, so did they! They did exactly what the Lord said.

That is all we have to do: do what He said! We do not need all the faith in the world. All the faith we need is to do what He said. We need faith to obey the Lord, and He will take care of the rest.

When the servant got to the house with the pitcher of water, Peter and John followed him into the house. They had "blind faith." They asked the servant, "Where is the master of the house?" The servant went for the owner. They asked him, "Where is your guest room?" It took a lot of grace to ask this of a stranger. It took a lot more than it does for us to invite someone to church. It took a lot more grace than it does for us to witness.

The owner pointed out the room to them, and they began to prepare it, telling him, "The Master is going to keep the Passover here." The owner just walked out, turning it over to them.

God controls natural things. Everything happens just as the Word says. It has nothing to do with our soul's salvation.

Someone asked Peter, "Do you and your master pay tribute?" Peter did not really know how to answer. He did not want to leave Jesus in a bad light with the assessors and collectors. He said, "Well, yes, we pay taxes." He went straight to Jesus to ask him about the matter. Jesus asked him, "Who pays tribute, the strangers or the children?" Peter answered, "Strangers." "Then the children are free," Jesus explained. Nevertheless, Jesus did not want to leave Peter in a bad light, and He does not want to leave us in one. He simply said to Peter, "Take your fishhook and go down to the lake. Bait your hook and throw it into the water. The first fish you catch will have some gold in its mouth. Take that gold and go pay the taxes."

His Word controls the natural. We can depend upon the accuracy of God's Word. Anything God says, we can count on it!

We have seen the accuracy of God's Word in the scientific world and in the natural realm. Now let us examine the accuracy of His Word as it relates to healing of the body.

Luke 7:1-10 tells us about a centurion who had a very good and dear servant in his service. This servant was dying. The centurion heard that Jesus was in the community. Since he was a Gentile he asked some of the elders of the Jews of the synagogue to go and ask the Master to come and heal his servant.

The elders went to Jesus and made the request. They said, "Master, we wish You would go. This centurion is a good man, and he is good to us. He built a synagogue for us to worship in. He is very kind to us. Master, we hope You can go." Jesus said, "All right. Let us go to him."

They started on their way to the centurion's home to heal the servant. Before they could get there, the centurion sent a friend to meet Jesus and tell him, "Master, my friend says that he isn't worthy for You to come under his roof. He does not feel worthy, and that is why he did not come to ask You. He, too, is a master. He says, 'Go' and people go. He says, 'Come,' and they come. He knows what it is like to have someone under his control. He said You do not have to come under his roof. All You have to do is just to speak the word and his servant will be healed."

Jesus turned around to look at his followers and said, "I have not found that kind of faith among you."

Is He finding that kind of faith today? Do we believe that all God has to do is say the word and it will be done? We look for proof. We want evidence. We want something to substantiate everything. But this man said that Jesus did not even need to come into his house, just speak the word.

God left His Word to us in James 5:14-15: "Is any sick among you? let him call for the elders of the church; and let them pray over him, anointing him with oil in the name of the Lord: and the prayer of faith shall save the sick, and the Lord shall raise him up." His Word has said it. Why do we not stand on it?

Jesus looked at those who had forsaken all to follow Him and He heard them say, "Here we are, Lord." He used them. He worked through them.

We have given up the world to follow the Lord. We are not out there in the world. We are not out there in the theater. We are not visiting drinking places. Neither are we in gambling houses. We are not found in the evil places of our respective communities. We pass up all of that to go to a dedicated sanctuary. We come there purposefully to worship God. Why cannot we turn our faith loose, and believe anything the Word says? Let us not ask questions, but just believe God's Word!

We were in a revival in the church I pastored. We had printed some handbills on the revival. The evangelist and his wife's pictures were on it, with the church name, address, phone number, pastor's name, and an invitation to attend. We distributed them over the city. A small stack was left lying on one of the altars. That night we asked if anyone would invest a three-cent stamp (yes, we could mail a letter for three cents then) in one of these handbills, put it in an envelope, address it to someone, and drop it in the mail. No one would know who mailed it.

The handbills all disappeared. The people did what we asked them to do. We met many people on the street who thanked us for the invitation. A prominent businessman and his wife attended. They enjoyed the music and singing, and believe it or not, the preaching! They came back for two or three nights in succession.

One night Mr. Tenney had a business engagement and

could not attend with his wife, so he told her that he would take her by the church and have Tom Fred, a sophomore in high school, to pick her up after church.

Tom was used to the church service being over at 8:00 to 8:15 in the churches he had gone to. We were just getting started when he got there. He came in and took a seat. When the altar call was given, he came up close to the altar. This was the first Pentecostal service he ever attended.

One of the men who knew his dad and knew Tom went over to him and said, "Let us explain what these people are doing," and explained Acts 2:38 to him. Tom said, "That is not in my Bible." The man said, "Oh yes, Tom, it is in your Bible." Tom answered, "Well, I've never read it." The man said, "It is still in there." Tom said, "I've gone to church all my life, and I've never heard that." With a smile the man repeated, "It is still in there."

Tom went home that night, got his Bible, and turned to Acts 2:38, and there it was! The next night Tom was back at the altar. Nothing but the Word of God moved him.

The Word of God is enough to move you. God does not owe you a knockdown like He gave Paul. He does not owe you a miracle. He has given you His written Word.

If someone refuses to believe the Word, he would not believe a person who had risen from the dead (Luke 16:31). If you will not heed the written Word, then you will not be convinced even if you heard the apostle Paul preach from the pulpit. Do something about what you already know.

Brother Tenney received the Holy Ghost! The Word led him.

The centurion said, "Just speak the word." Jesus said, "I have not found this kind of faith in all Israel." Then he said to the centurion, "Go, your servant is healed." When the centurion and friend got to his house, they found the servant healed! The accuracy of His Word—just as He said.

According to John 4:46-53, a certain nobleman lived in Capernaum, and his son was sick. He heard that Jesus was in Cana, an overnight journey's distance in those days. The nobleman did not send a servant to get the Master. His son was at the point of death, and he felt this mission was too important to send anyone else. In all probability he and his wife talked it over. Perhaps he went to the sickbed of his child and explained, "I am going after the Master to come and heal you." He left on that overnight journey. He arrived where Jesus was and asked Him, "Master, come and heal my son. He is sick unto death."

The answer did not happen the way he expected. Sometimes we have it in our minds just how we expect things to happen. But it may not work out that way. The nobleman thought Jesus would say, "All right, let's go," but Jesus looked at him and said, "Unless you see signs and wonders, you will not believe." The nobleman could have offered any argument. He could have said, "What am I doing here if I don't believe?" He could have said, "Why do you think I've traveled all night long to get here to ask You if I don't believe?" But he did not do that.

When I was seeking the Holy Ghost, a very dear lady would pray with me every night. She would kneel beside me and say in my ear, "Believe God, believe God." I wanted to look at her and say, "If I don't believe God, what do you think I'm doing here at this altar?" But someone does not receive the Spirit of God with an attitude like that. We have to get rid of that. That is the reason I did not receive the Holy Ghost that night.

Many people are waiting to see signs and wonders. We cry aloud, we are hungry to see signs and wonders, but Jesus does not owe us one. He is not going to show us anything just to convince us. He has chosen the preaching of the gospel to save those who will believe. Those who believe and are baptized will be saved. Those who do not believe will be condemned.

The Word of God says, "An evil and adulterous generation seeketh after a sign; and there shall no sign be given to it, but the sign of the prophet Jonas" (Matthew 12:39). No sign will be given but what has already been given: "For as Jonas was three days and three nights in the whale's belly; so shall the Son of man be three days and three nights in the heart of the earth" (Matthew 12:40). If we cannot believe in the virgin birth, the crucifixion, death, burial, and resurrection of Jesus Christ, He owes us nothing more than what He has already extended.

The nobleman stood there, looked at Him, and said, "Master, come, before my child dies." The Lord said, "Go, your son is healed." That is not what the nobleman asked for. He asked that the Lord come with him. When the Lord said, "Go, your son is healed," the nobleman did not say, "That was not what I was expecting." He did not ask the second time. He just turned and started walking toward his home. He was walking on the promise: "Go, your son is healed."

We do not walk by sight. We walk by faith. The nobleman was not walking by feeling. He was walking by faith: "Go, your son is healed." Night came with all that darkness brings—the crickets, the frogs, the snakes, the loneliness, the weariness of body, but he kept walking on the promise: "Go, your son is healed." No doubt every demon that could get to him whispered in his ear, "It didn't turn out as you thought it would." He kept standing on the promise: "Go, your son is healed." Perhaps another demon said, "You thought He cared for you enough to come with you, didn't you?" He kept walking on that promise: "Go, your son is healed."

We need to stand on the promises of God, or stop saying that we are. The nobleman kept on walking till midnight came. We can imagine how tired and weary he must have been by this time. We can visualize the lines etched on his brow from the worry over his sick son. This was not the way he had imagined things to turn out, but he kept walking as he ran the promise over and over through his mind: "Go, your son is healed." The morning dawned. He kept walking, turning the promise over again in his mind: "Go, your son is healed." The sun came up. He steadily walked on. Midday came. The hot sun beamed down upon him. His clothes stuck to his back with salty perspiration, but the promise was still alive to him: "Go, your son is healed."

By midafternoon he came within sight of his home. He saw someone running to meet him. No doubt the enemy put out one last desperate effort to kill his faith as he whispered into the nobleman's ear, "He is coming to tell you that your son is dead." When he got within shouting distance he heard his servant calling to him, "Your son is healed! Your son is healed!" As he reached the side of his servant the nobleman asked, "When?" The servant's answer is why we know it was a long, overnight journey. The man answered, "Yesterday afternoon at a certain hour." The nobleman knew it was just the hour that the Master said, "Go, your son is healed!" Accuracy! The accuracy of God's Word! When He says it, it is done!

I held a home missionary revival in Wheeling, West Virginia, years ago. There was no church of our faith in Wheeling at that time. Several people of Pentecostal faith were working in the town and were desirous of establishing a church there. A tent was erected, and the neighboring churches convened nightly. A young lady who was secretary and part-time nurse for a Jewish doctor invited him and his wife to attend the revival. They came and sat on the second seat with her. We secretly commended her for being a devoted Christian, and she must have been a faithful worker since her employer accepted her invitation. After I preached and extended the altar invitation, more people than ever before came up to pray with those at the altar. The prayer service was quite lengthy.

The Jewish couple continued to sit, looking on. Ten o'clock came. No one received the Holy Ghost. The Jewish doctor and his wife were still there at eleven o'clock. Soon afterwards they stood and walked out. They were no more than a block away when the altar service ceased. One of the ladies who had been in prayer came up and asked, "Do you know who was here tonight?" "Are you referring to the doctor?" I asked. "Yes," she replied, "I wanted someone to receive the Holy Ghost tonight so that they could see and hear someone speaking in tongues."

"What did you say?" was my startled reply. She repeated her statement. "I wanted them to see and hear someone receive the Holy Ghost."

"Is that why all of you were in the altar praying?" I asked.

"Well, that is why I was praying," she answered.

"That explains everything to me," I replied. "God does not grant the Holy Ghost on those terms. The Lord has never given the Holy Spirit just to prove to someone that He can. The only condition upon which God will fill with the Holy Ghost is when a person repents and seeks Him with all his heart. God will answer him regardless of who is or is not there." He did not owe the Jewish doctor anything. God is indebted to nobody.

Someone once made a request for another person and placed more emphasis on that person's body than on the soul. What is the Lord more interested in? Keeping the sun in its place, the earth on its course with everything operating smoothly in the scientific kingdom, securing a colt for the Master, paying taxes for Peter, healing the centurion's servant and the nobleman's son—all of which are in the natural or physical kingdom—or is He more interested in saving a soul for whom He died?

Our Lord Jesus Christ did not die to place this world on course. He placed it on course in the beginning of time. Our Lord Jesus did not die to untie a colt from a hitching post. He did not die to put gold in a fish's mouth for Peter to pay taxes with. He did not die to heal a centurion's servant and a nobleman's son. There was healing in the physical kingdom before Calvary. But He died to save your soul!

Jesus came not to establish a scientific kingdom. "In the beginning God created the heaven and the earth" (Genesis 1:1). He did not come to establish the natural and physical kingdom. It was all here before Calvary.

He came to establish a spiritual kingdom! That is what He gave His life for!

There are not enough demons in and out of hell to keep you from receiving the promise of God if you will stand on the Word and believe it! It is yours for the asking. It is yours for the receiving! "And I say unto you, Ask, and it shall be given you; seek, and ye shall find; knock, and it shall be opened unto you. For every one that asketh receiveth; and he that seeketh findeth; and to him that knocketh it shall be opened" (Luke 11:9-10).

Let us see the accuracy of God's Word in the spiritual kingdom. On the Day of Pentecost the waiting believers were gloriously baptized with the Holy Ghost. (See Acts 1-2.) A crowd gathered, wondering what was taking place. When Peter heard them say, "These men are full of new wine," he stood and explained, "These are not drunken, as ye suppose, seeing it is but the third hour of the day. But this is that which was spoken by the prophet Joel; And it shall come to pass in the last days, saith God, I will pour out of my Spirit upon all flesh" (Acts 2:15-17).

Peter preached about Jesus, and the crowd cried out to Peter and the rest of the apostles, "What shall we do?" (Acts 2:37). That is all God is waiting for you to ask.

Peter's answer was to repent, be baptized, and receive the Holy Ghost. That very day about three thousand people obeyed his words and were added to the church.

It all came to pass exactly as God had said through His prophets. The accuracy of His Word.

Acts 10 tells the story of devout, dedicated, God-fearing, money-giving Gentiles. In Acts 10:1-6 we read of one of them:

There was a certain man in Caesarea called Cornelius, a centurion of the band called the Italian band, a devout man, and one that feared God with all his house, which gave much alms to the people, and prayed to God alway. He saw in a vision evidently about the ninth hour of the day an angel of God coming in to him, and saying unto him, Cornelius. And when he looked on him, he was afraid, and said, What is it, Lord? And he said unto him, Thy prayers and thine alms are come up for a memorial before God. And now send men to Joppa, and call for one Simon, whose surname is Peter: he lodgeth with one Simon a tanner, whose house is by the sea side; he shall tell thee what thou oughtest to do.

God gave a vision to Peter down in Joppa to prepare him to visit Cornelius and present to him the message of salvation. Peter walked into Cornelius's home and said, "I perceive that God is no respecter of persons: but in every nation he that feareth him, and worketh righteousness is accepted with him" (Acts 10:34-35).

God had heard Cornelius say, as he fell at Peter's feet, "We are so glad you are here. We are ready to hear whatever is commanded you of God."

Peter gave out the same plan for salvation that he had preached at Pentecost: "Repent, and be baptized every one of you in the name of Jesus Christ for the remission of sins, and ye shall receive the gift of the Holy Ghost. For the promise is unto you, and to your children, and to all that are afar off, even as many as the Lord our God shall call" (Acts 2:38-39).

The Lord knew the heart of Cornelius and these people. He was so ready to fill them with the Holy Ghost that while Peter was yet preaching, the Holy Ghost fell on all those who heard the Word, before they were baptized.

The Spirit fell on those who heard the Word. It happened just as God said it would.

In a revival meeting in one of our churches, a young man and his wife came in and sat on a back pew. The next night they were back, and they kept coming for several nights.

One night the young man arose and came to the altar. Most of the time the wife comes first and the husband follows, but this time it was the husband who came and knelt and prayed. That lady got very angry with him. She began to talk quite loudly about what she was going to do when she got him home. He was earnestly praying and did not hear her threats. People gathered around him and started praying with him. The lady was in the back of the church still making threatening remarks, puffing, pouting, and spouting off. The kneeling man had his head buried in his hands on the altar.

He was progressing in prayer, and suddenly he raised his head up with his hands over his head. The woman became more angry. She stood up, began walking up and down, and declared what she was going to do. All of this she did because the man was seeking God. The praying man fell over on his back, and she ran down the aisle to him, placed her hands around his head, and started trying to drag him down the aisle! While she was pulling on him, he began to speak in tongues as the Spirit of God gave the utterance. She turned loose of him as if he were on fire and ran to the back door!

This incident shows that it matters not how close the devil may be around: he cannot keep us from receiving the blessing of God. God's Word is true! It is proven. It is accurate.

God is more interested in the souls of mankind than He is in the sun rising in the morning. He cares more for souls than for anything else He created. If the Word is accurate regarding everything else in the world, how much more is it so with the salvation of the soul!

We are living in troubled times. Atomic weapons can destroy us all in a matter of minutes. Yet we have something to stand on: the promise of God. It undergirds us. What else is there to stand on? The Word of God is sure. We can put our trust in God and in the accuracy of God's Word!

7

DEFEATING THE ENEMY WITH HIS OWN WEAPON

I Samuel 17:48-51

Outline

Introduction: Many people are of the opinion that David slew Goliath with a stone. This assumption cannot be proved scripturally.

I. David and Goliath
    A. Goliath's boasting and defiance of God
    B. The defeat of Goliath
        1. Felled by the sling and stone in the name of the Lord
        2. Head severed by his own sword
    C. The Philistines' flight and Israel's pursuit

II. Is Satan Unaware God Can Take His Weapon to Defeat Him?
    A. Never underestimate the tactics of the enemy
    B. Satan is defeated

III. Abraham, Isaac, and Jacob

IV. Moses

V. Job

VI. Daniel
    A. The three Hebrews
    B. Daniel's steadfastness

VII. Esther

VIII. Jesus
 A. Jesus' baptism and wilderness experience
 B. Jesus' ministry
 C. Jesus' death

 IX. New Testament Church
 A. Day of Pentecost
 B. Persecution of the early church
 C. Paul
 D. John

 X. Conclusion
 A. Christ is Lord of history
 B. In every instance, God wrested the weapon from the enemy's hand and defeated him on his own territory!

DEFEATING THE ENEMY WITH HIS OWN WEAPON

And it came to pass, when the Philistine arose, and came and drew nigh to meet David, that David hasted, and ran toward the army to meet the Philistine. And David put his hand in his bag, and took thence a stone, and slang it, and smote the Philistine in his forehead, that the stone sunk into his forehead; and he fell upon his face to the earth. So David prevailed over the Philistine with a sling and with a stone, and smote the Philistine, and slew him; but there was no sword in the hand of David. Therefore David ran, and stood upon the Philistine, and took his sword, and drew it out of the sheath thereof, and slew him, and cut off his head therewith. And when the Philistines saw their champion was dead, they fled (I Samuel 17:48-51).

This passage of Scripture introduces the subject we want to deal with: wresting the weapon from the enemy's hand and defeating him on his own territory.

Many people are of the opinion that David slew Goliath with a stone. This assumption cannot be proved scripturally. When David slung the stone, it hit the giant in the forehead, stunned him, and knocked him out, and he fell down. David had no sword in his hand. He ran to the fallen giant, drew the sword from its sheath, and severed the giant's head with his own sword.

This is the sword Goliath carried about, boasting about what he had done with it and what he was going to do with it. The Israelites had seen the sword glistening and glittering in the sun as Goliath boldly displayed it and said, "Choose you a man for you, and let him come down to me. If he be able to fight with me, and to kill me, then we will be your servants; but if I prevail against him, and kill him, then shall ye be our servants, and serve us. . . . I defy the armies of Israel this day; give me a man, that we may fight together" (I Samuel 17:8-10).

When Saul and all Israel heard those words of Goliath, they were dismayed and greatly afraid.

Goliath should not have defied God's chosen. Little did he dream that God was going to take his weapon right out of his hand and defeat him on his own battlefield. God is able to do that! We extol and highly praise our God for His unlimited power. We bow to and serve only the greatest!

Let us see how little Satan is and how weak when confronted with God and His unlimited power. May we realize that God can take the weapon right out of the enemy's hand and defeat him on his own territory at his own game!

David's victory over Goliath was not enough. Goliath's defiance of God's army had to be answered. Let us notice Goliath's boasting and David's response to him:

And the Philistine said to David, Come to me, and I will give thy flesh unto the fowls of the air, and to the beasts of the field. [Watch what you say, Goliath. It may return to you.] *Then said David to the Philistine, Thou comest to me with a sword, and with a spear, and with a shield: but I come to thee in the name of the LORD of hosts, the God of the armies of Israel, whom thou hast defied. This day will the LORD deliver thee into mine hand; and I will smite thee, and take thine head from thee; and I will give*

the carcases of the host of the Philistines this day unto the
fowls of the air, and to the wild beasts of the earth; that
all the earth may know that there is a God in Israel
(I Samuel 17:44-46).

The Lord could have allowed the stone sent in His
name to finish off Goliath. But God had a greater victory
for David and Israel! Why not allow David to do to the
giant what the giant had boasted of doing to David: feed
his flesh to the fowls of the air and to the beasts of the
field?

When David knocked the giant out, ran to him, took
Goliath's own sword, and cut off his head, the Philistines
fled—they ran as cowards do! The men of Israel shouted
and pursued and killed them from Sharim to Gath to
Ekron. David took the head of the Philistine and brought
it to Jerusalem.

If God guided the stone sent by David in the name
of the Lord and allowed the giant to be knocked out, it
could have killed Goliath right then and there. But God
had a greater victory in mind. He wanted Israel's army
and all the world to know, see, and hear that He can wrest
the weapon out of the enemy's hand and defeat him on
his own battleground! The Philistines were humiliated,
embarrassed, and put to open shame, reproach, and
despair.

God also leaves to us in His Word an example in David
of what He can do with an individual who is completely
consecrated, dedicated, willing, and sold out to Him and
His cause.

We must never underestimate the tactics of the
enemy or his boldness in attacking us and the cause of

God. Nevertheless, we have access to God's unlimited power through prayer. If we are prayerful, if we are given to prayer, the enemy of our soul can never trap us.

How many times has God taken the weapon out of our enemy's hand and defeated him for us? Perhaps there are times when we do not even realize all that He is doing for us.

Let's go to the Book of Beginnings and read the promises God made to Abraham:

Now the LORD had said unto Abram, Get thee out of thy country, and from thy kindred, and from thy father's house, unto a land that I will shew thee: and I will make of thee a great nation, and I will bless thee, and make thy name great; and thou shall be a blessing" (Genesis 12:1-2).

Abram departed as the Lord had told him to do. This was a long and arduous journey that spanned many miles and years of Abram's life. Many changes were wrought in his life.

Abram was perhaps around thirty-five years of age and married to Sarai when they departed Ur of the Chaldees to go into the land of Canaan. Numerous trials and testing came his way. Satan hindered many times. But God's hand was upon his life, and God is all-seeing and all-knowing. Abram's day would come! God would bring him through with a high and mighty hand!

At Haran he buried his father, Terah. Abram was seventy-five years of age when he departed from Haran.

Then came the day he found himself on the plains of Moreh among the Canaanites. The Lord spoke to Abram again, telling him, "Unto thy seed will I give this land,"

and there he built an altar to the Lord (Genesis 12:7).

At the next move he pitched his tent near Bethel. There he built an altar and called upon the name of the Lord.

Under trial Abram forsook the place of blessing, because of famine, and stayed in Egypt for a time. He almost lost Sarai to Pharaoh, but a truce was made between the two houses. In Genesis 13 Abram returned to the place where his tent had been at the beginning, to the place of the altar in Canaan.

He now found that he had to separate from his nephew, Lot, because of strife between their herdsmen. Satan is the author of strife. Abram's heart was greatly troubled as Lot took his first step in backsliding when he pitched his tent toward Sodom. Lot made friends with the wicked men of Sodom and took a second step in backsliding. Where there is strife, there is every evil work (James 3:16).

Now the Lord said to Abram, after Lot was separated from him, "Look! All the land you see, I will give to you and to your descendants after you."

Then Abram removed his tent and dwelt in the plain of Mamre in Hebron. There he built another altar of sacrifice, confirming the Abrahamic covenant: the land given by the Lord God and the natural posterity promised to him (Genesis 13:16). After Abram overcame everything that would retard him, God rewarded him by giving him more than he had before.

Lot caused another great trial for Abram. Because of war he was called upon to rescue this wayward nephew and family.

The Lord blessed Abram to know him as the "most

high God, possessor of heaven and earth" (Genesis 14:22). Melchizedek the priest brought forth bread and wine and blessed Abram. This revelation made a remarkable impression upon Abram, and he gave Melchizedek tithes of all. The king of Sodom offered spoil to Abram. He answered, "No, lest you should say, I have made Abram rich." Abram was God's man; Satan could not buy him.

"After these things the word of the LORD came unto Abram in a vision saying, Fear not, Abram: I am thy shield, and thy exceeding great reward. . . . In the same day the LORD made a covenant with Abram, saying, Unto thy seed have I given this land" (Genesis 15:1, 18).

Sarai bare no children, so she gave Hagar, her Egyptian maid, to Abram, and Ishmael was born. (See Genesis 16.)

Abram was getting up in years. Satan tried him repeatedly. He plagued him by reminding him, "You have no heir by Sarai. You are too old for children. And don't you wish that you could stop moving? As soon as you get settled you have to move again. Why do you have to do that? Move . . . move. . . ." Nevertheless, "by faith Abraham, when he was called to go out into a place which he should after receive for an inheritance, obeyed, and he went out, not knowing whither he went" (Hebrews 11:8).

The revelation of God as El-Shaddai, Almighty God, came to Abram when he was ninety years old! God changed his name to Abraham and made the Abrahamic covenant everlasting. He established circumcision as the sign of the covenant. He told Abraham, "As for Sarai thy wife, thou shalt not call her name Sarai, but Sarah shall her name be. And I will bless her, and give thee a son also of her: yea, I will bless her, and she shall be a mother of nations; kings of people shall be of her" (Genesis 17:16). Satan, you might as well give up. Defeat is coming your way!

Abraham was ninety-nine years old and Ishmael was thirteen when they were circumcised.

In the plains of Mamre, Abraham entertained the Lord. They talked about the promised heir. This couple was so old now. Sarah laughed at the thought. They were told, "Is anything too hard for the Lord?"

God then revealed to Abraham that He would destroy Sodom and Gomorrah. Abraham became an intercessor. When ten righteous people could not be found the cities were destroyed, but God saved Lot and his two daughters. (See Genesis 19.)

Abraham suffered a lapse at Gerar. He posed Sarah as his sister. Abimelech took her, but God told him, "She is a man's wife." Therefore Abimelech sent her back. Restoration and healing were granted in answer to Abraham's prayer. (See Genesis 20.)

Finally, when Abraham was one hundred years old, Isaac was born! The enemy did not like the celebration that took place at his birth, but what could he do?

There came the day when God called upon Abraham to offer Isaac as a sacrifice. By this time Abraham was convinced, after all he had received from God, that the Lord was in control! Satan could not make him doubt. "He staggered not at the promise of God through unbelief" (Romans 4:20). What do you think about that, Satan?

The death and burial of Sarah took place when she was 127 (Genesis 23:1). After the death of Sarah, Abraham married Keturah (Genesis 25:1).

Abraham had one son by Hagar. Abraham had one son by Sarah, and he was the promised heir.

He had six children by Keturah (Genesis 25:1-2; I Chronicles 1:32). This was a total of eight children to start the fulfillment of the Lord's promise: "If a man can number the dust of the earth, then shall thy seed also be numbered" (Genesis 13:16).

Let us notice the promise in Genesis 15:18: "Unto thy seed have I given this land, from the river of Egypt unto the great river, the Euphrates." Rapid growth occurred in this area with Ishmael and his descendants. Ishmael was over fourteen years older than Isaac. He was married and had a family before Isaac was old enough to take a wife. God said that Ishmael was to be a nation, too (Genesis 17:20).

Friction and quarreling in the Middle East started with Sarah and Hagar over their sons (Genesis 21:9), and the boys took it up later. The enemy had a heyday when this started. The enemy is filled with elation as he views the results down through the years.

But oh, Satan, just wait. God will call a halt. The day is coming when "the kingdoms of this world are become the kingdoms of our Lord, and of his Christ" (Revelation 11:15).

Abraham, the friend of God, lived to secure Rebekah as a bride for Isaac. He died at the good old age of 175 years (Genesis 25:7).

As we see from this resumé of Abraham's life, God over and over confirmed to him the promise and covenant He made to him. In spite of the unfavorable circumstances, God started a nation of people through him.

God likewise brought Isaac and Jacob through many things. He reaffirmed the covenant to Isaac. Yet we read of two sons, two only, Esau and Jacob, born to Isaac.

From Esau, his sons, and grandsons were the people of Edom (also called Seir), or Edomites, and the Amalekites. (See Genesis 36.) The Scripture enumerates the kings of Edom before the kings of Israel because Esau was born first.

Jacob was born second. God later changed his name to Israel. He fathered the twelve tribes of Israel, and God reaffirmed the promise to Israel (Genesis 35:10-12).

The grandsons of Israel bring us into the fourth generation: Abraham, Isaac, Jacob, and Joseph. The promises and covenant were still active. They did not die with Abraham!

Satan knew about the promise that God made to His friend. The enemy bitterly attacked that family. He would have been better off had he never come against God's chosen. In his blindness and foolishness he did his best to tear that family apart. The weapons he used then are the same he uses today, as we shall see.

The lives of Isaac, Jacob and Esau, and Joseph were filled with pioneer work of those primitive days—adventure, romance, love, happiness, hate, goodness, remorse, poverty, riches, failure, success, the good way of the heavenly walk with God, and the way of destruction. Esau threatened to murder Jacob, and Joseph was tricked by his brothers. Satan used the weapons of jealousy, envy, strife, malice, murder, betrayal, lying, selling, and deceit against them.

Little did the devil know when he successfully placed it into the hearts of Jacob's sons to sell Joseph that it would open the door for the family of God to become a great nation. The devil did not know that he was assisting the efforts of God in getting this family into the land of Goshen in Egypt, where they would have plenty of food and would rapidly multiply. Evidently Satan did not remember or understand God's Word:

And he said unto Abram, Know of a surety that thy seed shall be a stranger in a land that is not theirs, and shall serve them; and they shall afflict them four hundred years; and also that nation, whom they shall serve, will I judge: and afterward shall they come out with great substance. And thou shalt go to thy fathers in peace; thou shalt be buried in a good old age. But in the fourth generation they shall come hither again (Genesis 15:13-16).

If Satan had remembered these words he never would have caused Joseph to be hated and rejected by his brothers, sold to the Ishmaelites who carried him to Egypt, and sold to Potiphar. How did Satan feel when he heard Joseph reassure his brothers? He told them, "Be not grieved, nor angry with yourselves, that ye sold me hither: for God did send me before you to preserve life. . . . It was not you that sent me hither, but God: he hath made me a father to Pharaoh, and lord of all his house, and a ruler throughout all the land of Egypt. . . . Go up to my father, and say unto him, . . . Come down unto me, tarry not" (Genesis 45:5, 8-9).

A total of seventy people, all of Jacob's family, now dwelt in Egypt. (See Genesis 46.) Satan probably laughed again and again at their persecution during the 430 years they were there. (See Exodus 12:41.) But wait . . .

From a beginning of seventy souls, the total family of Jacob, some biblical scholars estimate that Moses led from two and one-half to three million souls out of Egyptian bondage! Who gets the last laugh? Not Satan.

What would Satan have done had he realized he was only assisting the efforts of God? The Lord is not the author of confusion. When confusion happens He can turn it to His advantage.

Let us consider the life of Moses. The growth of Israel was so great that Pharaoh and his cabinet became alarmed. What if Israel should overthrow the Egyptian government? If a nation should invade, or if Egypt declared war, the Israelites could very easily ally with the enemy. The Egyptians decided to destroy all male children born to the Israelites.

A man of the house of Levi took to wife a daughter of Levi, who bore a son. She hid him three months, until she could no longer hide him. She waterproofed an ark of bulrushes, put the baby therein, placed it in the reeds by the river's brink, and posted his sister to watch what should happen to him. Pharaoh's daughter came to bathe, saw the ark, and had it brought to her. When she saw the child as it wept, she had compassion on him. God gave her a love for the child! The babe's sister said to Pharaoh's daughter, "Shall I go get a nurse of the Hebrew women, that she may nurse the child for you?" At the woman's bidding, she called the child's mother. The child grew, she brought him to Pharaoh's daughter, and he became her son. She named him Moses, "because I drew him out of the water." (See Exodus 2:1-10.)

All right, devil, watch this: Moses received the best of everything that the palace afforded. He could have inherited a throne. Instead the Scripture says, "By faith Moses, when he was come to years, refused to be called the son of Pharaoh's daughter; choosing rather to suffer affliction with the people of God, than to enjoy the pleasures of sin for a season; esteeming the reproach of Christ greater riches than the treasures in Egypt: for he had respect unto the recompense of the reward" (Hebrews 11:24-27).

Only God can so beautifully slip the weapon out of Satan's hand and defeat him with his own intrigue, and He does not have to make a second attempt to accomplish what He wishes.

God led Moses into a desert country, talked to him, prepared him, and sent him back to Egypt to lead his people out. That is the same baby boy the enemy thought he could put to death!

Has it ever occurred to you that were it not for the plans and schemes of Satan we may not have the Book of Job? Job 1:6 tells us that the sons of God came to present themselves before the Lord, and Satan came also among them. Had Satan not been there to accuse, there is a chance we would not have the Book of Job, because the entire book was written about the devil's attack that God permitted him to make on Job.

The Book of Job has been used to comfort many hearts. When a person's back is to the wall, when he has lost everything, we can always take him to this book. Satan can see that his plans and schemes went awry, for God blessed the latter end of Job more than his beginning.

We have this great record all because Satan accused, and it backfired on him! His plan did not have the desired and expected effect! If Satan could only learn. . . . The

Book of Job gives us one of the greatest proofs of the resurrection. Would we have this record if Satan had not attacked Job?

Let us move to the Book of Daniel for an example of God taking Satan's weapon and defeating him with it. King Nebuchadnezzar dreamed a dream and forgot it. He demanded his magicians, astrologers, sorcerers, and the Chaldeans to show the king his dream and the interpretation. They argued that no one could do such a thing! The king was furious and commanded the destruction of all the wise men of Babylon.

Daniel heard about it. He asked the king to give him time so he could show the king the interpretation. Daniel went to his house and had his three Hebrew brethren to ask the mercies of God for them and his fellows that they not perish.

The secret was revealed to Daniel, and he gave to the king the forgotten dream with the interpretation. The king promoted Daniel and make him ruler over Babylon and chief over all the governors. At Daniel's request, the king set Shadrach, Meshach, and Abednego over provincial affairs, but Daniel sat in the gate of the king. Daniel told the king that no wise men can give such secrets, but God reveals them and makes them known. (See Daniel 2.)

Nebuchadnezzar made an image of gold and decreed that all should worship it or be cast into a fiery furnace. (See Daniel 3.) Someone tattled: the three Jewish boys refused to worship the image. The king in fury demanded they be brought to him. "If you do not worship, you shall be cast into the furnace, and who shall deliver you out of my hand?" demanded the king.

Shadrach, Meshach, and Abednego answered, "O

Nebuchadnezzar, our God is able to deliver us from the fiery furnace, and he can deliver us from your hand, but if not, we will not serve your gods, nor worship the golden image."

They were thrown into the fiery furnace heated seven times hotter than before. Mighty men bound Shadrach, Meshach, and Abednego in all their clothes and threw them in. The flames of the fire killed the men who threw them in! The three Hebrews fell down bound into the furnace.

Nebuchadnezzar was astonished! Quickly he arose. (He had a ringside seat!) He spoke with his counselors, "Did we not cast three men bound into the fire?"

They answered, "True, O king."

The king said, "Lo, I see four men, loose, walking in the midst of the fire, and they have no hurt; and the form of the fourth is like the Son of God" (Daniel 3:25).

He went to the mouth of the burning furnace, and called out, "Shadrach, Meshach, and Abednego, ye servants of the most high God, come forth" (Daniel 3:26).

Everyone saw that the fire had no power upon them. No hair of their head was singed, neither were their clothes changed, and they had no smell of fire on them.

Then Nebuchadnezzar spoke, "Blessed be the God of Shadrach, Meshach, and Abednego, who sent His angel and delivered His servants who trusted Him. Therefore, I make a decree: Every people, nation, and language who speak against their God shall be cut in pieces and their houses made a dunghill, because only their God can do this." Then the king promoted them.

We know many people who have gone through fire but who came out stinking forever after. The smell of fire is all over them wherever they go. If they go to camp meeting, they talk about the fire they were in. At conference, they are in the lobby telling how they were mistreated and used. You can smell them all over the place.

How much better it is to meet people who can come out of the fire with no smell on them. If anyone ever finds out they have been in the fire, someone else has to tell it. They worship and thank God for deliverance.

Surely the devil wished that he had backed off and left the Hebrew boys alone! God can and does take the weapon from the enemy's hand and defeats him with it. Did Satan ever learn this lesson? No, never, he tried again.

In Daniel 6, when Darius became king, we learn that Daniel was preferred above all the presidents and princes, because an excellent spirit was in him, and the king wanted to set him over the whole realm. Then the presidents and princes sought to find fault with Daniel and prevent this.

It would have been the best thing in the world for them to have recognized the working of Satan and subdued their jealousy. It would have been better for them to leave Daniel alone in the position he was in, for in the end they were punished and Daniel obtained a better position.

These plotters said, "We can't find any fault against Daniel. He is faithful to the province. There is no error in him. If we find something it will be with his laws concerning his God." That is what Satan helped them to find and do.

"O King Darius, live forever," they flattered him. "Make a decree that whosoever shall ask a petition of any god or man for thirty days, except you, O King, he shall be cast into the den of lions." King Darius signed the decree.

Now let us watch the Lord take Satan's weapon out of his hand and defeat him at his own game.

Daniel knew the law was passed. It did not affect his worship and prayer life. Just as he had always done, he went into his house with the windows open, kneeled and prayed three times a day, and gave thanks to God.

The men spied on him; they found him praying and making supplication before his God. They hurried to tell the king, "Daniel does not respect you. He does not regard you or your decree."

When the king heard their words, he was greatly displeased with himself. He set his heart on Daniel to deliver him.

The plotters pressed their point: "O King, no decree or statute which the king establishes may be changed."

The king had to save face. He commanded Daniel to be cast into the lion's den, but the king had confidence in Daniel's faith and said, "Daniel, this God whom you serve continually will deliver you." Daniel must have been an effective missionary. The king went to his palace and spent the night fasting. He arose early, went in haste to the den of the lions, and called, "O Daniel, servant of the living God, has He delivered you from the lions?"

Daniel answered, "O King, live forever. My God sent His angels to shut the lions' mouths. They have not hurt me. Innocence was found in me, and before you, O King, I have done no harm."

The king was very glad! He had the men who accused Daniel cast into the den of lions. The lions ate them before they came to the bottom of the den.

Satan, you cannot burn them, and the lions will not eat them! Can you not see that God can take your weapons out of your hands and defeat you on your own territory?

The end of the story is this: "Then king Darius wrote unto all people, nations, and languages, that dwell in all the earth: . . . I make a decree, That in every dominion of my kingdom men tremble and fear before the God of Daniel: for he is the living God, and stedfast for ever, and his kingdom that which shall not be destroyed, and his dominion shall be even unto the end" (Daniel 6:25-26).

Do you have regrets, Satan, that you ever attacked Daniel, God's man? Your attack resulted in the decree that everyone fear the God of Daniel. Do you not wish you had left him alone? You have been bested and have lost another weapon. Well, you asked for it!

Let us pick up another example from the Old Testament. King Ahasuerus made a feast for all his princes of the provinces, his nobles and other rulers, both great and small. Vashti, the queen, also made a feast for the women in the royal house.

On the seventh day the king had drunk so much wine that he was feeling reckless. He wanted all the men to see and admire his beautiful wife. Ahasuerus sent a servant to get her.

The queen refused to come because she knew the king's request was unwise. It was contrary to the customs of the people.

The king was very angry. He and his cabinet decreed that Vashti come no more before the king, and her royal estate be given to another. (See Esther 1.)

In the kingdom was an orphan by the name of Esther.

Esther was only a little girl when both her parents died, and her cousin Mordecai took her to live with him. Esther became like a daughter to him. He worked in the king's household to earn their living. Both Mordecai and Esther were Jews. Who in the world would ever think that the royal estate would be given to her? But God was going to place someone there whom He could use to deliver His people. God has done so many things that surprise everyone. He asks no one about what He wills to do.

Did Satan cause the drinking king to send for Vashti? He now wishes that the king had never sent for her.

In the 127 provinces there were wealthy governors with beautiful daughters. They were happy to spend lavishly for them to become queen. The king commanded throughout the kingdom that the most beautiful young women should be brought to the palace. He would choose the one he liked best for his queen. (See Esther 2.)

Mordecai knew Esther was very beautiful. He believed she would make a good queen. When the young women from all parts of the kingdom came to the palace, Mordecai sent Esther too. He advised her, "Don't tell anyone we are related or that you are a Jew."

When Esther was brought before the king, he knew at once that she was the one he wanted. Ahasuerus placed the royal crown of Persia on Esther's head.

One day Mordecai overheard two men planning to kill the king. He sent word to Esther at once. She sent a servant to tell the king. The king found the report was true, and the two men were put to death. A record was written of how Mordecai had saved the king's life. The king forgot to promote the loyal gatekeeper. He never suspected Mordecai the Jew was his wife's relative.

One of the princes at the palace was proud Haman, who was very rich, and he knew how to please the king. At Haman's passing through the gate all the servants except Mordecai bowed low before him. Mordecai refused to bow before any man and give him the honor that belonged to God. As a result Haman wanted to punish him.

Haman planned to kill the Jews. One day he told Ahasuerus, "O King, there are certain people scattered throughout your countries who obey their own laws instead of yours. This is not good. Let a law be made to kill these people." Little did he know Queen Esther was a Jewess.

Under the king's seal Haman sent letters to the rulers that on a certain day all Jews were to be put to death. Haman thought he would get even with Mordecai now. (See Esther 3.)

Queen Esther became very troubled, for one day Mordecai did not pass by her window. Quickly she called for the advisor the king had given her and sent him to find out what was wrong with Mordecai. Mordecai sent him back to tell Esther, "Go to the king and plead for your people." Esther was afraid. How could she go to the king unless he called for her?

Mordecai sent Esther this word: "Do not think you will escape death just because you live in the palace. Who knows, perhaps you have come to the kingdom for such a time as this!" In the meantime, the Jewish people all fasted and prayed three days. (See Esther 4.)

On the third day Esther went to see the king. He loved her, so he held out the scepter. She knelt before the throne and touched the scepter.

"Queen Esther, what is your request? You shall have it up to half of my kingdom," Ahasuerus said.

"O King, if it pleases you, let the king and Haman come tomorrow to a special dinner I will have for you."

Haman felt honored to be the only guest invited to eat with the king and queen. But his gladness turned to anger when he passed the gate and Mordecai did not bow.

That night King Ahasuerus could not sleep. He had a servant read from the book of records. It was in the records about Mordecai's warning of the two men who plotted to kill the king.

"What honor was given Mordecai for this?" the king asked.

"Nothing," the servant answered.

The king heard someone in the court. "Who is it?" he asked.

"It is Haman," the servant reported.

"Let him come in," the king said. Then he asked Haman, "What shall be done for the man the king delights to honor?"

Haman thought the king meant him. He said, "Let the man be dressed in your royal robes, ride on your horse, and wear your crown. Have a prince go before the honored one and call out for all to hear, 'This is done for the man the king delights to honor.'"

"You are my noble prince. Be sure you do everything you said for Mordecai, who saved my life," the king told Haman.

Haman was so upset he forgot the invitation to dine with the king and queen. The king had to send for him. (See Esther 6.)

At dinner the queen told the king, "If I have found

favor with you, O King, and if it pleases you, save my life and the lives of my people. We are all about to be killed!''

Imagine the king's astonishment. "Who would dare to threaten the queen's life?'' he asked.

"The man is Haman,'' answered the queen.

Haman just thought he had been frightened before. Never had he guessed the beautiful queen was a Jewess. Haman sat speechless.

The king stormed out to his garden wondering how to punish Haman. When he returned and found Haman begging for his life, he ordered the servants, "Hang Haman on the gallows he prepared for Mordecai.''

To this day the Jews keep the Feast of Purim to commemorate their deliverance, and they tell how Queen Esther saved the lives of her people.

God did it again! It is nothing for him to take Satan's strongest weapon from him and whip him with it.

God is full of surprise moves! No one in the world, not even Samuel, thought David would be anointed king. His own father did not give him a chance. Samuel had Jesse, David's father, to send for David.

Who would say the Messiah would be born into an humble carpenter's home? Despite all the grand palaces around, he was born to a carpenter's family. God knew who would listen to Him. God knew who would obey Him. He knew who would shelter and protect the baby Jesus.

It was just unthinkable that the Lord would give the keys to the kingdom to a fisherman! There were many lawyers, philosophers, doctors, and other educated people around. With God it is not what is on the outside, but what is in the man!

When Jesus was born, Satan's priority was to destroy

him. When the wise men came to Jerusalem asking, "Where is He that is born King of the Jews?" Herod was troubled. "What can this mean? What if this newborn king should take away my throne?" Secretly he told the wise men, "When you have found Him, let me know that I may come and worship Him!" That was the furtherest purpose from his heart.

When Herod put out the edict to kill all the male babies, God spoke to Joseph to take Mary and the babe down to Egypt. He instructed them to stay there until He gave the word.

This event fulfilled a type found in Hosea 11:1, which says, "I . . . called my son out of Egypt." God fulfilled that verse of Scripture and took care of Satan without half trying. It is so easy for our God to take care of things, if we will only let Him. He is always a step ahead of the enemy! He can make Satan's weapon ineffective before he can begin!

When John the Baptist baptized Jesus in the Jordan River, a voice from heaven said, "This is my beloved Son, in whom I am well pleased" (Matthew 3:17). Satan heard, and those words did not sound good to him.

Immediately after His baptism the Spirit led Jesus into the wilderness, where he fasted forty days and nights. (See Matthew 4:1-11.) Satan remembered the heavenly voice. No doubt he thought to himself, This is my big chance. He is very weak from fasting. I'll fix him. He won't be so well-pleasing after this.

No, Satan, never! Jesus is never weak! If He can experience a weak moment, He is stronger, greater, and mightier than Satan at his best!

"If you are the Son of God . . ." Satan tempted.

After three rounds Satan was miserably defeated, and Jesus launched the greatest ministry the world has ever seen. He scored the greatest victory over the devil. He was now ready to do His Father's work.

After Satan lost the battle in the wilderness where Jesus so strongly triumphed over him with the Word, Satan forever knew and recognized him.

On one occasion when Jesus came into the country of the Gadarenes, he met a poor man possessed with demons. Satan trembled! The man screamed out, "What have I to do with thee, Jesus, thou Son of God most high? I beseech thee, torment me not" (Luke 8:28). The demons knew and recognized Jesus.

"Jesus asked him, saying, What is thy name? And he said, Legion: because many devils were entered into him" (Luke 8:30). They offered no argument. They knew they were going! They were no match for Jesus.

And they besought him that he would not command them to go out into the deep. And there was there a herd of many swine feeding on the mountain: and they besought him that he would suffer them to enter into them. And he suffered them. Then went the devils out of the man, and entered into the swine: and the herd ran violently down a steep place into the lake, and were choked (Luke 8:31-33).

We marvel at the man's having so many demons and being able to live. The swine could not stand them! They would rather be drowned.

Let us notice what Mark 1:32-34 records:

And at even, when the sun did set, they brought unto

him all that were diseased, and them that were possessed with devils. And all the city was gathered together at the door. And he healed many that were sick of divers diseases, and cast out many devils; and suffered not the devils to speak, because they knew him.

Not only did they know Him, they were subject to Him!

In Mark 1:21-26 we read:

And they went into Capernaum; and straightway on the sabbath day he entered into the synagogue, and taught. And they were astonished at his doctrine: for he taught them as one that had authority, and not as the scribes. And there was in their synagogue a man with an unclean spirit; and he cried out, saying, Let us alone; what have we to do with thee, thou Jesus of Nazareth? art thou come to destroy us? I know thee, who thou art, the Holy One of God. And Jesus rebuked him, saying, Hold thy peace, and come out of him. And when the unclean spirit had torn him, and cried with a loud voice, he came out of him.

After Jesus' temptation in the wilderness where He so completely subdued the devil, the devil forever knew Jesus. Demons cried out at Jesus' approach and begged for mercy, even reminding Jesus, as if He did not know, "Art thou come hither to torment us before the time?" (Matthew 8:29). The devil always knows Jesus, and he knows when his time is up!

The Gospels record the temptation of Jesus in about A.D. 26. The Acts of the Apostles records another incident dated about A.D. 56:

And God wrought special miracles by the hands of Paul: so that from his body were brought unto the sick handkerchiefs or aprons, and the diseases departed from them, and the evil spirits went out of them. Then certain of the vagabond Jews, exorcists, took upon them to call over them which had evil spirits the name of the Lord Jesus, saying, We adjure you by Jesus whom Paul preacheth. And there were seven sons of one Sceva, a Jew, and chief of the priests, which did so. And the evil spirit answered and said, Jesus I know, and Paul I know, but who are ye? (Acts 19:11-15).

Satan cannot be defeated by Satan, but Satan acknowledged knowing Jesus, and the apostles of Jesus! He had no power over them. We have the same power within us. The works of Satan are subject to the followers of Jesus through His name.

Jesus went about doing good. He made friends, called His followers, turned water into wine, healed the crippled, taught the people, walked on the water, calmed the storm, raised the dead, cast out demons, restored sight to the blind, fed the multitudes, and forgave and saved sinners.

Satan could not stand it! He still thinks he can destroy Him! He will try again. Satan, it would be better for you if you would just leave Him to His good works.

After the prophets left us the recorded words concerning Jesus' miraculous birth, there are ministers in pulpits who do not believe in Jesus' virgin birth. Even worse, they teach others not to believe. That is Satan's work, blinding people to the truth, but millions do believe the virgin birth.

Satan stirred up strife, envy, and even caused some to accuse Jesus of blasphemy. They denied that He was God (John 10:33).

Who, other than God, can forgive sin? No one. Jesus forgave sins. He was God manifested in the flesh. (See I Timothy 3:16.)

Well, they put Him to death. They crucified Him and laid Him in the grave. After three days He arose.

Before He ascended He told His disciples to "tarry in the city of Jerusalem, until ye be endued with power from on high" (Luke 24:49). He had many followers, but how many obeyed?

He fed four thousand followers in Mark 8:1-9. On another occasion where he fed the multitude there were five thousand men present, besides the women and children (Matthew 14:21). Many followed Him. Was it for the fishes and loaves? How many obeyed His last instructions? After Jesus' beautiful ministry with all His good works and great teaching we find 120 in the upper room waiting for the promise (Acts 1:15).

Satan was happy on the day of Jesus' death and burial, but how did he feel at the close of the Book of Acts?

And when the day of Pentecost was fully come, they were all with one accord in one place. And suddenly there came a sound from heaven as of a rushing mighty wind, and it filled all the house where they were sitting. And there appeared unto them cloven tongues like as of fire, and it sat upon each of them. And they were filled with the Holy Ghost, and began to speak with other tongues, as the Spirit gave them utterance (Acts 2:1-4).

This experience of the 120 was the beginning of the first church in Jerusalem. We can read the results in the Book of Acts. Acts 2:41 tells us three thousand souls were added to them that day. Verse 47 says, "And the Lord added to the church daily such as should be saved."

The devil stirred up persecution against the church. The first wave of persecution gave Peter the opportunity to address the Sanhedrin. (See Acts 4:1-21.) The devil did not realize he could do nothing against the truth, but only for it!

The second persecution brought the apostles into court (Acts 5:17-42). In verse 33 the religious leaders took counsel to kill them. An influential teacher of the law, Gamaliel, warned them not to. They beat the apostles, commanded them not to teach in the name of Jesus, and let them go.

The third persecution brought Stephen's address to the council and resulted in his death. (See Acts 6-7.)

Saul was the chief figure of the fourth persecution (Acts 8). What happened? Two great things took place. First, as Acts 8:4 tells us, "Therefore they that were scattered abroad went every where preaching the word." They became the first missionaries, preaching Jesus Christ and Him crucified. Philip went to Samaria. Peter and John joined him. Philip baptized the Ethiopian.

The second great event was that Saul the persecutor was converted and became Paul the apostle to the Gentiles! Satan was again defeated with his weapon, this time the weapon of persecution.

As we continue reading about the outreach of the church we lose count of the number of believers before we conclude the Acts of the Apostles. When we get to the last verse of the last chapter of Acts, we can write these words below it: "To be continued!" Only heaven has the count!

The devil is not so glad now. In fact he is miserable! Not only did he fail to destroy the Jews, but now the Gentiles are partakers of salvation.

If Satan can read, what does he think about Ephesians 4:8-10? After Jesus' resurrection, He descended into the lower parts of the earth and led captivity captive, and that is not all. To the church He gave gifts to continue His work!

Jesus' works are greater after His death and resurrection than before! But we must remember: He will work for us only as much as we allow Him to.

The enemy's persecution put Paul in prison many times. This only gave him time to write and leave us the Pauline Epistles. What were the results for Satan?

John's exile on Patmas probably entailed hard labor in the island's quarries. Some Christians had been killed. Others were imprisoned for their faith. Worse was yet to come. Early Christians eagerly expected Christ's return, but sixty years after His death this hope was yet unrealized. It was only human for some to waver.

God is in control no matter how things may look. So, in spite of the conditions for John on Patmos, he wrote: "I was in the Spirit on the Lord's day" (Revelation 1:10).

Christ is the Lord of history. He is coming again. He reassures us through John and gives future events for all the world. John's message not only inspires and instructs but encourages all to keep fighting the good fight of faith.

We started in Genesis, came through the Prophets,

through the Gospels, into Acts with the record of the first church, into the Epistles, and to the Book of Revelation. We have shown our Lord and Savior wresting the weapon from the enemy's hand and defeating him on his own territory in every instance. The church continues to be ever victorious!

8

EQUAL CHANCE
Luke 23:39-43

Outline

Introduction: In this passage of Scripture we find the perfect will of God being done, giving all people an equal chance.

I. The Will of God Relative to the Crucifixion
   A. Faced with going to the cross Jesus prayed, "Not my will, but thine, be done" (Luke 22:42)
   B. God "spared not his own Son, but delivered him up for us all" (Romans 8:32)
   C. Fulfillment of the will of God as stated in prophecy (Isaiah 53)
   D. Scoffers and mockers are like the ant in a story

II. It is the Will of God for All Men Everywhere to Have an Equal Chance
   A. One thief who died with Jesus was saved
   B. The other thief died lost within reach of Christ; His chance was equal to the other

III. Others with Equal Chances
   A. Using a six-shooter to invite a man to church
   B. Ruth and Orpah
   C. The rich young ruler
   D. The blind beggar
   E. The woman with the issue of blood
   F. The twelve spies
   G. Zacchaeus
   H. Judas

IV. The Church Was Established and Commissioned to
Evangelize the World (Acts 1:8)
A. To give all people an equal chance
B. The church has not failed us
C. The way

Conclusion: The chance is all you are promised. You have
that chance. Take advantage of your chance.

EQUAL CHANCE

And one of the malefactors which were hanged railed on him, saying, If thou be Christ, save thyself and us. But the other answering rebuked him, saying, Dost not thou fear God, seeing thou art in the same condemnation? And we indeed justly; for we receive the due reward of our deeds: but this man hath done nothing amiss. And he said unto Jesus, Lord, remember me when thou comest into thy kingdom. And Jesus said unto him, Verily I say unto thee, To day shalt thou be with me in paradise (Luke 23:39-43).

To those who love God and trust in His Word with abiding faith and hope, this is a beautiful reading. To the heart of the student probing the depth of this passage, it yields many avenues of thought. Let us identify a few.

First, we would not go amiss in using this portion of Scripture to portray the perfect will of God as given in Romans 8:32 and Hebrews 2:9-10. We can see God's perfect will being done.

Jesus prayed in the Garden of Gethsemane for three hours at different times. At intervals He would awaken the sleeping disciples to watch and pray with Him as He went back to pray another hour. He prayed, "Father, if thou be willing, remove this cup from me: nevertheless not my will, but thine, be done" (Luke 22:42). He drank the cup, subduing the human will in order to have no will but God's. To be ready to stand, to stay, to go, to wait, to suffer, to yield, to say, "Not my will but thine" is the last conquest of grace, and we see Jesus in the perfect will of God.

Looking at another avenue of thought, in this scriptural passage we find the fulfillment of much prophecy. The following prophecies from Isaiah 53 were fulfilled in the death of Jesus:

- He was numbered with the transgressors (verse 12).
- He had no form nor comeliness, no beauty that we should desire Him (verse 2).
- He was despised and rejected, a man of sorrows, acquainted with grief, not esteemed (verse 3).
- He was smitten and afflicted (verse 4).
- He was wounded and bruised, and the iniquities of all were laid on Him (verses 5-6).
- He was brought as a lamb to the slaughter, and as a sheep before shearers is dumb, he did not open his mouth (verse 7).
- He made His grave with the wicked and was with the rich in His death (verse 9).

All of these prophecies and others we see fulfilled in Jesus as He hung suspended on the cross between two thieves. Under the cross the soldiers parted lots for His garments. He was on the cross when they pierced His side.

The thought we want to introduce now is not explicitly stated in this passage, but it is suggested: It is God's will that all people everywhere have an equal chance to be saved.

Let us picture the three crosses on Golgotha. Jesus hung on the middle cross. On either side of Him was a thief on his respective cross. Both were in reach of Jesus! Even though this scene was horrifying in its depiction, yet we can say, "It is beautiful," when we grasp what was taking place there.

One of the malefactors—we do not know which, for the Scriptures do not tell us which side of Jesus' cross he was on—one of these transgressors railed on Him. What does the word "railed" mean, as used here when it is stated, "One of the malefactors . . . railed on him"? To rail means to speak abusively, using bitter, scornful, reproachful language.

When we read the things he said to Jesus, we can grasp the full significance of the situation. Can we imagine a mere man, a thief no less, speaking in such a manner to Jesus, the only One who could help and save him? He challenged Jesus with these words: "If you are who you say you are, save yourself and us. Come down from the cross."

It is important to note that Jesus completely ignored everything this malefactor said. Jesus gave him no attention at all. Surely the thief derived no pleasure from his tirade, since Jesus ignored him and his abusive language.

We sometimes wonder what attention some of the boasters, cursers, scoffers, and challengers get from God. Some years ago it was reported that some Soviet cosmonauts came back from space and in a very derisive manner said, "Where is God? At no time did we see Him up there." Had they asked, we could have told them before they looked that they would not see Him. God pays no attention to mockers.

Mockers are like the ant in the following story. A little ant moved to a crosstie on a railroad track. There he built his home in a crack of the crosstie. He was very cozy and snug in his new home until a train came down the track, shaking the ties, the rails, the track, and all the earth around him. It almost tumbled him from his bed, but he stayed with his home.

One of his neighbors from his old ant neighborhood came to visit him and inquired in their ant language how he was faring and if he liked his new home.

The little ant answered, "My home is just fine. It is warm and cozy. I like it here except for one thing. Ever so often, some huge, dark contraption of a thing comes rolling down these tracks, shaking the whole world. It almost shakes me out of my bed. I have to hang on for dear life. Oh! That monstrous thing frightens me so! What shall I do?"

With disbelief written all over his face, his friend said, "I don't believe that! I never heard of such a thing."

"Well, it is so anyhow," the little ant declared.

They continued talking about it until they began to argue. Finally the friend made what was to him a very profound declaration: "I will prove to you that it isn't true!" He put action to his words and crawled upon the rail, placing himself in the center of it. He threw out his tiny chest and dared that monstrous thing to come running the track!

Of course, no railroad company is going to dispatch a train and send it roaring down the track just to prove to a little ant that it is real and does run the rails. All the little ant had to do was just sit there on the rail. On schedule a train would come!

The ant in this story is like some foolish people who dare God to do certain things just to prove to them His existence. God also moves on schedule! Scoffers, skeptics, and boasters can go on with their sneering and daring. They get no attention from God now, but just wait! On schedule He will intervene!

The malefactor railing on Jesus received only silence from Him. Did Jesus even look at him?

The other evildoer was so taken aback he said to the first, "Don't you fear God? Don't you have any fear at all of God in your heart? We are justly due what's coming to us, but this Man has done nothing at all to merit what He is going through." Then he turned to Jesus and asked, "Lord, remember me when You come into Your kingdom."

He got the attention of the Lord!

When people turn to Him as this man did, they can count on getting Jesus' attention. He heard Jesus say to him in such tender tones, "Today you will be with me in paradise." He called and Jesus answered.

It could have been so for the other man. Both were there under the same situation, under the same conditions. Each of them were within reach of Jesus with an equal chance.

Three men hung on three crosses:

One died *in* sin—the unrepentant. He was lost!

One died *out* to sin—the repentant. He was saved.

One died *for* sin—Jesus. He is the Savior for all.

Yes, the penitent thief was saved. No, he was not baptized in Jesus' name, and he did not receive the Holy Ghost. He did not have the privilege afforded us. He died under Old Testament conditions. Jesus was not yet dead. The penitent died on the other side of the crucifixion. The thief, though he was granted repentance, could not receive God's greatest gift, because he was on the wrong side, the other side of Calvary. At that time the commission to baptize in Jesus' name and the gift of the Holy Ghost was yet future.

In connection with this point, we need to understand that the Gospels form a bridge connecting the Old Testament with the New Testament. We could say they are the crossing over from the Old to New Testament.

The theme of the whole Bible is Christ. In the Old Testament we find the preparation for Christ. In the Gospels we find Him manifested to the world. The Gospels record His appearance to mankind, calling and teaching of the disciples, resurrection, and ascension. In the Book of Acts He is preached and His gospel propagated in the world. In the Epistles His gospel is explained. In Revelation God's purposes in and through Christ are consummated. With this understanding, we can see how the penitent thief was saved.

"God is no respecter of persons" (Acts 10:34). He is "not willing that any should perish, but that all should come to repentance" (II Peter 3:9). It is very interesting to note that the phrase "all should come to repentance" is for all people through all ages of time. Though there are different conditions to be met at various stages in God's economy, yet repentance is granted to all. "For godly sorrow worketh repentance to salvation" (II Corinthians 7:10).

It is God's will for everyone to have an equal chance of being saved. It is the will of God for you, for me, for everyone to have a chance to be saved. That is all we are promised of God. That is all we will receive from God—a chance to be saved. Then it is left up to us as to whether or not we take advantage of that chance.

That is all the church can give you—a chance! The church can offer you that chance, but there is no law in God's Word, there is no law in the church, there is no law existing that will force you to serve God.

I had a very interesting experience while conducting a revival that beautifully explains the phrase "force you to serve God." It was Friday of the fourth week of revival. The meeting was coming to a close. A young couple with an ardent love for souls came to me, the evangelist, and said, "We have the nicest of neighbors. We have been inviting them to church. We haven't succeeded yet. We believe that if you will go with us tomorrow and invite them they will come."

I said, "Surely, I will go with you. Be glad to."

Saturday morning we walked upon the porch and rang the doorbell. The couple came to the door and invited us in. I summed up the situation in a glance. They both worked through the week. This was their day to do laundry and clean the house.

The couple invited us to sit down.

"No," I said. "I see you are busy. If we monopolize your time, we'd ruin your day and defeat our purpose in coming here." Instead of being seated, my next words were, "Say, friend," and already I felt they were friends. They were so kind, pleasant, and congenial. They had created a wonderful atmosphere in welcoming us. So I felt free to speak. "Say, friend. You know what I would do about 8:30 in the morning, if the law of your state allowed it, and God permitted it?"

Now I had not planned to make the preceding statement. I really did not know exactly what I was going to say next, but I had started, and I could not back out of it even though I was becoming embarrassed because of the trend my thoughts were taking me in the conversation. So I repeated, "Do you know what I would do about

8:30 in the morning, if the law of your state allowed it, and God permitted it?''

"What's that, Reverend?'' was the respectful response.

I heard my answer: "I'd come to your house in the morning about 8:30 with a six-shooter.'' The little couple accompanying me began looking at pictures on the wall. "I would go to your bedroom with that six-shooter, put it in your ribs, and say 'Ole boy, get out of this bed. You are going to church with me today.' I would take you to church, sit you down, and force you to stay there while I would go to the pulpit and preach to you. Then I would put the six-shooter back in your ribs, and say, 'Get in that altar and repent.' I would hold you there until you had repented. I would then put the six-shooter back on you and take you to the baptistery and baptize you in Jesus' name. I would take up my six-shooter, take you back to the altar, and say, 'Don't leave this altar until you receive the Holy Ghost and speak in tongues.' After that, my friend, every time I would meet you on the street of gold in eternity, you would hug my neck and say, 'Reverend, I bless the day you came to my house with the six-shooter.' ''

The little couple who brought me now had their backs turned. I felt they must be wishing they had not asked me to come. To tell the truth, I too was beginning to wish I had not come. I had to conclude this most unusual conversation. I heard my voice say, "Friend, we can't do that. The law doesn't allow it. If the law of man permitted, God would not allow it. He wants no one forced to serve Him. So, we have done all we can to give you a chance to be saved. Some years ago a man burdened for souls came to your city, built and established a church. He felt it was revival time again. Ads in the newspapers, handbills, and invitations have been extended. We have preached a four-week revival. The lights of the church will be on tonight. The doors will be open. Now we have come to your house to extend to you the warmest, most cordial invitation we know how to extend. Please come to the house of God tomorrow. Good day." Silence permeated the room.

We walked out. The couple who brought me followed me to the car and took me home without saying one word.

I got out of the car feeling terrible. Why in the world did I say all that? But I had said it. I felt a complete failure.

I did not see them anymore. They did not come. I closed the revival on Sunday night and left to hold a revival in another state.

Two weeks from the night I left, I received a call from the pastor. "Say, do you remember the couple that you talked to about the six-shooter?"

"Yes, I most certainly do. I've been trying to forget," I answered.

"Oh, no, no, no! Don't say that," the dear pastor replied. "We baptized the man and his whole family tonight. When I asked him to say something he told the whole church about you and the six-shooter."

The man testified, "It opened my eyes to the realization that if I am ever going to be saved, and my family saved, *I* will have to do something about it. No one can force me to. No one can do it for me. Everything in the world that can be done for me to be saved has been done. It is now left up to me."

After our visit, he had talked it over with his wife, repeating almost verbatim our conversation. "Good people came to our city and built a church years ago. We have never been in the church. They brought in an evangelist. They have been in a four-week revival. The evangelist came to our home to invite us. Now, if we are going to be saved there is something for us to do. Everyone else has done their part. It's up to us."

Joyously he concluded his testimony: "Here we are. We are so happy."

Twelve years later I was speaking in the camp meeting in that district. After preaching I was still up front. A giant of a man came down the aisle with a big smile on his face, but I did not know him. The first time I had seen him he was in work clothes. This well-dressed man came right up to the platform as though he were at home there.

As he put out his hand to grasp mine, his greeting was, "My evangelist friend! I came to hug your neck on this side of eternity before we get to the street of gold. I want to tell you that I bless the day you came to our house and talked to us about the six-shooter. It opened my eyes."

Needless to say I was equally happy and could now be happy about that strange conversation. Never before or since have I been led that way. I am glad I submitted to what I felt, even though I doubted that God had anything to do with that conversation. God knows how to get His man!

Oh yes, the man became the Sunday school superintendent of his church and a lover of souls.

In the Old Testament we find two people whose chances were equal, with no differences in their chance whatsoever. They are Ruth and Orpah.

Elimelech and Naomi with their two sons, Mahlon and Chilion, moved down into Moab to escape a famine. Elimelech, Noami's husband, died. She was left with her two sons. They took wives of the women of Moab. One was named Orpah and the other Ruth. Mahlon and Chilion also died, leaving Naomi with two daughters-in-law for whom she felt responsible.

Naomi heard the famine had lifted in Israel, and she thought it best now to return home. She talked it over with her daughters-in-law, not one at a time, but both at the same time. She showed no favoritism. Both heard everything she had to say.

The time came for her departure. The three set forth on the journey. They walked part of the way on the road. Naomi stopped and said to both of them, "Go back to your mother's house. Go back to your people. The Lord grant that you may find rest, each of you, in the house of a husband."

They lifted up their voices and wept. Orpah and Ruth both said, "No, let us go with you."

Naomi continued to reason with them. "Were I to marry tonight and have sons, would you wait for them till they are grown?"

They lifted up their voices and wept again. Then Orpah kissed her mother-in-law, but Ruth cleaved to her. Orpah went back. She faded forever out of the picture, never to be heard again.

Noami continued to reason with Ruth, "Your sister-in-law has gone back to her people. You go too."

But Ruth said, "No. Don't send me away. I don't want to leave you."

"Ruth, we Jews have only one God. Gentiles worship

191

many gods," was Naomi's answer.

"Your God shall be my God," declared Ruth.

Naomi realized that Ruth was determined. She had made up her mind. She knew what she was going to do.

"Well, I don't know where we are going to live. If we die, we don't have a burying place," Naomi told her.

Ruth said, "I'll live wherever you live. I'll be buried wherever you are."

Naomi said no more. She started walking toward Israel, and Ruth followed right behind her. We know the rest of the story and the godly inheritance that came to Ruth.

Naomi had no respect of persons with her daughters-in-laws. Orpah could have done exactly as Ruth. She had the same chance. Ruth's chance was no better. Naomi did not drive Orpah back. Equal chance was there for both.

Let us go to the New Testament for another person who let his chance slip away. A rich young ruler came to Jesus and asked, "Good Master, what shall I do that I may inherit eternal life? I know the commandments. I've kept them from my youth up."

"Well, one thing you still lack," Jesus answered. "Sell what you have, give it to the poor, and come follow Me."

Now this young man had great possessions, and he loved them more than he loved God. He went away sorrowful.

What a chance the young man had. He had an audience with the Creator. He talked with Him about inheriting eternal life. Yet he let his most wonderful chance slip. (See Matthew 19:16-22; Luke 18:18-23.)

This is the only record we have where God ever gave this specific command to anyone. God knew where this man's heart was and what his god was. When we come to God, to really find Him, we learn if there is anything we love more than God. We cannot serve God and mammon (Matthew 6:24).

Let us take a look at another scene. There was an old blind beggar sitting by the roadside outside of Jericho. He did not have one dime. If he had a friend, where was he? His ears were very keen. He heard footsteps, not just one, but more like a parade. There was a crowd of people approaching!

Now the footsteps started passing by. "What does this mean?" he cried out to anyone who would listen to him.

Someone was kind enough to say, "Jesus of Nazareth is passing by!"

The beggar thought, Jesus of Nazareth. I've heard of him. He cares for people. He heals! Here is my chance! He began to cry out so loudly and so desperately that one following the Lord went over to him and said, "Quiet down! You must not disturb the Master. You don't have to yell like that!"

The blind man realized, I may not have another chance. I will not let this one slip. He cried the louder, "Jesus, son of David, have mercy on me!"

Jesus felt the desperation of the beggar's heart as He heard his cry. He stopped and commanded, "Bring him here."

I have always wondered who tried to hush the beggar. Was it one of the disciples? Whoever he was, I hope he was the one Jesus told to bring the beggar to Him.

Jesus stood still and said to him, "What do you wish for Me to do for you?"

He answered, "Lord, that I may receive my sight."

"Immediately he received his sight, and followed him, glorifying God." (See Luke 18:35-43.) He used his chance when he realized that he also had an equal chance.

A little woman with an issue of blood for twelve long years had spent all her living trying to get well. When she heard of Jesus and His works, she said, "If I can but touch the hem of his garment, I shall be whole."

Doing so was quite an undertaking—a problem for her. She had been ill for twelve years. She was probably stooped from weakness through the loss of blood. This was her only hope, so she determined that somehow she would touch Him. We can imagine how she did.

A crowd of people gathered in her vicinity to see Jesus. The stragglers and latecomers passed her by. She kept walking slowly. Finally she was on the edge of the crowd, but she was too weak, too tired, to elbow her way through the mass of people.

She dropped to the grass to rest a moment and retain her breath. Lying there she realized she could get through! There is more room down by these feet, she thought.

She started crawling. What an arduous task it must have been for her. Finally she was there behind Him. The trembling hand reached out. Lightly she touched the border of His garment. Immediately her issue of blood was staunched. (See Luke 8:43-48.)

Now she was troubled by the next words she heard Jesus say: "Who touched Me?"

When everyone denied doing so, Peter and those who were with him said, "Master, in this pressing throng of humanity anyone could have touched you."

Jesus explained, "It was not a bump, or an ordinary push or touch. Somebody has touched Me, for I perceive that virtue (healing) has gone out of Me."

The woman realized that she was not hidden, so she came trembling. Falling down before Him she declared to Him before all the people why she had touched Him and how she was immediately healed.

Jesus' answer to her was, "Daughter, be of good comfort. Your faith has made you whole." She had a chance. He came to her community. She went where He was. She took advantage of her chance.

Don't go into eternity with a memory of having a chance and letting it slip.

Twelve spies were sent to spy out Canaan. All were honest, brave, and good men, or they would not have been sent on such an important venture. They all had the same blood ties to Abraham. They all ate the good fruit they found in the promised land.

Ten came back with a bad report: "We are as grasshoppers in the sight of those giants." Why did their faith and determination fail them? Two brought back a good survey and outlook: "We are well able to possess the land."

All had the same opportunity and privilege to perform a good work. Only two took advantage of faith and the promise of God. Ten said, "We cannot." Two said, "We can." All had an equal chance.

Zacchaeus heard the wonderful reports of the people. Jesus had entered and was passing through Jericho! Everyone was headed for Jericho! Zacchaeus longed to see Jesus. He was so short of stature he thought, I don't have a chance in that crowd.

It has been said, "Where there's a will, there's a way." Zacchaeus believed this. He ran before the crowd, climbed up in a sycamore tree, and thought, I will really see Him as He passes under this tree!

Jesus knew Zacchaeus. He granted him an even greater pleasure than this little tax collector could ever have dreamed. When Jesus came to the place under the tree, He looked up and said, "Zacchaeus, come down. I want to visit with you at your house."

Really, did Zacchaeus have the same chance as the other people? Of course. Jesus knew his desire and provided an equal chance!

Was Judas born to betray the Lord? No! He was not ordained to such an end. He had the same opportunity as the other eleven disciples. All were given an equal chance.

God gives everyone an equal chance. He created the world and all that is in it. He made man in His image to have fellowship with Him. Man failed God. God made a way through Jesus and His crucifixion to reestablish communion with man. The church was established and commissioned to evangelize the world, thus giving all people an equal chance.

God went to unlimited length to establish a true church to search out men's souls. The church doors are open, giving us an equal chance.

Has God or the church failed you? No! A thousand times no! The church has and is giving you a chance to be saved. It has not, as yet, reached all the world, but it has reached you. Does anyone have a better chance than you to be saved? God's Word gives you an equal chance.

Heaven and earth will pass away, but God's Word will

forever stand. "He that believeth and is baptized shall be saved; but he that believeth not shall be damned" (Mark 16:16). "Then Peter said unto them, Repent, and be baptized every one of you in the name of Jesus Christ for the remission of sins, and ye shall receive the gift of the Holy Ghost. For the promise is unto you, and to your children, and to all that are afar off, even as many as the Lord our God shall call" (Acts 2:38-39).

Compiler's Note

Brother Glass preached the message "Equal Chance" over one hundred times around the world beginning at "Jerusalem, . . . Samaria, and unto the uttermost part of the earth."

We have no way of knowing how many times this message was taped and retaped. He never cared that it was copied. He always felt, "Let the Word go forth." He had very strong feelings that this is a message that God would have all to hear and be saved.

Brother Glass prayed the following prayer the last time he preached "Equal Chance" in the First Pentecostal Church of DeRidder, Louisiana, at the request of Pastor Rex Johnson on August 27, 1989.

Our Father, our heavenly Father, our Lord and our God, You are loving the people of this congregation tonight through Your servants on this platform. You loved them enough to go to Calvary for them. You became the propitiation of sin for them. You want them to have the chance You provided for them. You want them to be saved.

We have tried, O God, as You reached for them. We

have done all we can tonight to extend the chance to be saved to the lost of this congregation. We pray, Father, that You will help them to act on their chance and not let it slip by.

Someone in this world just the age of each and every one here is now slipping into eternity while we stand in this place of the holy for You, Father, to reach their souls. They are fighting death as they go out into an endless eternity, but we are here, alive, with a chance to be saved. We pray for the lost, O God, in Jesus' name! Amen.